Contents

IV

Immigration &

Published in Sydney by
  The Federation Press Pty Ltd
    PO Box 45, Annandale, NSW, 2038.
    71 John St, Leichhardt, NSW, 2040
    Ph: (02) 9552 2200 Fax: (02) 9552 1681

National Library of Australia Cataloguing-in-Publication

  Burnley, I. H. (Ian Harry), 1939- .
  Immigration and Australian cities.

  Bibliography.
  Includes index.
  ISBN 1 86287 258 9.

  1. Cities and towns - Australia. 2. Infrastructure (Economics) - Australia. 3.
  Immigrants - Housing - Australia. 4. Australia - Emigration and immigration.
  I. Murphy, Peter, 1949- . II. Fagan, Robert H. (Robert Harold), 1947- .
  III. Title.

307.3160994

Typeset by The Federation Press, Leichhardt, NSW.
Printed by Ligare Pty Ltd, Riverwood, NSW.

The authors

Ian Burnley is an Associate Professor in Geography at the University of New South Wales. Peter Murphy is an Associate Professor in Urban Planning at the University of New South Wales. Robert Fagan is Professor of Geography at Macquarie University.

Although the authors collaborated on the structure of the book and reviewed each other's material, prime authorship was as follows: Fagan wrote Chapter 7, Murphy Chapters 4, 5, 6 and 8, Burnley Chapters 2 and 3. The Introduction (Chapter 1) and Conclusion (Chapter 9) were written jointly.

Acknowledgments

This book is a revised and expanded version of a study prepared for the Australian government's Bureau of Immigration, Multicultural and Population Research (BIMPR) in 1996 as part of its commitment to the International Metropolis Project of the United States and Canadian governments. The work is published with permission and we are grateful for this having been granted. The authors would especially like to acknowledge Dr John Nieuwenhuysen, Dr Lyn Williams and Ms Fiona McKenzie, all formerly of the BIMPR and its predecessors. We, particularly Burnley and Murphy, worked with the Bureau on a variety of projects from 1989. The Bureau's program was not an easy one to pursue given the intrinsically politicised nature of the immigration debate. But we always appreciated the dedicated professional work of the Bureau's staff with whom we were involved. We would also like to acknowledge the competent and energetic research assistance of Alan Jenner, Kate Tribe and Neil Pfister, of the University of New South Wales, without whom the depth of research and information on which the book is founded would not have been possible.

List of figures

List of tables

chapter one

Introduction

Immigration has become a basic feature in all highly developed countries of the world . . . Several factors contribute to this growth of international migration as a global process: (a) unequal levels of development between receiving and sending countries; (b) the growing internationalization of all developed economies; (c) major changes in the organization of the economy and of labour markets in advanced economies which have created multiple opportunities for the incorporation of immigrants . . . Internationalisation is particularly important in the current period. It creates bridges with other countries – bridges initially designed to be travelled by capital flows but eventually also travelled by immigrants. When these bridges connect highly developed countries this immigration is largely of professionals; when they connect with less developed countries, you have labour migration. Both types of flows are constitutive elements of that which we call the global economy. (Sassen 1995, p. 53)

It is a truism that Australia is a country of immigrants. The indigenous population were originally migrants and immigration has played an important role in population growth since formal European settlement began. Indeed since 1788, more than 9 million persons have migrated to Australia. Much of this began with the gold rushes in the 1850s, since the non-indigenous population of Australia was as few as 400,000 in 1850. From its inception, Australia became a highly urbanised nation, despite the rural, outback and 'bush' ethos. Immigration contributed to this urbanisation from the days when former goldfields miners, prospectors, engineers, labourers and entrepreneurs flooded back to the embryonic colonial capital cities. The immigration surges of city dwellers and rural labourers from Britain and Ireland in the 1880s, 1900s and 1920s was also strongly focussed on the cities as was the great expansion of immigration after the Second World War and the associated development of ethnic diversity in the migration flow.

1

Since the Second World War alone, more than 5.3 million immigrants have settled in Australia. In the same period some 1 million persons have emigrated, either Australia-born seeking a new life overseas, or immigrants and their Australia-born children returning home or elsewhere. On a per capita basis Australia has conducted, since the late 1940s, what has been by international standards a very substantial immigration program. Australia has the highest proportion of immigrants in its population of any nation in the world apart from Israel. In the mid-1980s, net overseas migration stood at 0.76 per cent per annum of the Australian population. Contemporaneous figures for Canada and the Federal Republic of Germany – other high immigration nations – were 0.35 and 0.26 per cent respectively (Murphy 1993). Over the same period debates, backed by argument and information of variable quality, have been conducted and re-conducted on the economics of immigration and its social and cultural aspects. Wooden et al. (1994c) have comprehensively reviewed much of this discourse.

Debates about immigration

From an economic perspective, in the broadest sense debate is centrally concerned with the net economic benefits that Australia derives from immigration. There are both longer and shorter run perspectives on this question. Moreover, the context within which debates are conducted has shifted significantly over time as Australia's economic fortunes have waxed and waned and as the basis for economic growth has shifted. Assessing the existence and extent of net economic benefits is difficult and leaves room for perennial debate among economists.

In the longer term the immigration program has been regarded as being essential to building up Australia's labour force so as to enable businesses to meet domestic and international demand for goods and services, thus leading to national economic growth. Immigration itself adds substantially to domestic demand. In the 1950s and 1960s this line of argument carried particular weight when the concern was primarily to obtain low-skilled and semi-skilled labour for the factories and construction industries and parts of the then relatively small service economy. This was a period when manufacturing output and employment grew substantially, largely to meet the needs of an increasingly affluent Australian population rather than for export. These were the years of the 'long economic boom' when, due to the rising affluence of the population, there was massive expansion in the provision of new housing built at low densities on the fringes of the cities. Demand for building materials and the appliances needed to furnish a modern house were a major spur to industrial production. So too was burgeoning demand for private automobiles which was both the product of rising affluence and a major influence on the explosion of low density suburbanisation.

In the 1990s immigrants are no longer needed to provide cheap labour for the factories because employment opportunities in manufacturing were decimated during the period of de-industrialisation in the 1970s and 1980s. Rather the need now – if there is one – is to fill vacancies in the service sector. There are two broad and strongly contrasting types of service jobs. Much the largest category includes low skilled personal services jobs, such as taxi driving, household cleaning and child care, and in the lower echelons of the tourism and recreation industries. Far fewer in number are opportunities for skilled managers and professionals and for those running their own businesses.

Whereas in the 1950s and 1960s unemployment was virtually non-existent, as an outcome of national economic restructuring and slow economic growth since the early 1970s it is now the number one social problem in Australia. Immigration has regularly been scapegoated as 'taking jobs away from Australians'. This perception has been fuelled by the reality of very high levels of unemployment among certain groups of recent immigrants. The question has been asked with increasing stridency in recent years, 'Why should we be taking any immigrants at all when unemployment is such an intractable problem?'

In addition to fuelling growth in the work force, a key argument used to justify Australia's high immigration program in the 1950s and 1960s was the need to increase the size of the domestic market for goods and services. The idea was that a larger population would encourage businesses to increase in size and to diversify their range of production. Increased size of businesses creates what economists term 'economies of scale', which basically means that goods and services can be produced more cheaply. This, so the argument went, would lead to job growth and decreased reliance on imports of manufactured goods. The argument, however, has much less force today with the increased globalisation of markets. Firms, according to this revisionist position, do not need to rely on domestic markets for their livelihoods since the world is potentially their oyster. Similarly, the economies of scale argument is less persuasive – though still relevant in some parts of the economy – because today's system for producing goods relies much more on flexibly specialised, smaller and medium-sized firms rather than the very large manufacturing plants of yesteryear.

Setting aside the question of unemployment, which is obviously a key social concern in Australia, the major cost factors associated with immigration derive from demands placed on governments to provide infrastructure and services. The issue here is not so much the extent of that demand, which can be estimated by simple arithmetic, but whether or not, through their contribution to the national taxation base as workers and business proprietors, immigrants cover the public costs that they generate.

Another issue associated with immigration concerns its possible impacts on inflation. This possibility arises from additional demand for goods and services which, if that demand cannot easily be met by suppliers, will result in price inflation; especially house prices. When suppliers, especially governments, have to borrow money to build infrastructure, that may also result in higher interest rates which may in turn depress economic activity.

The subject of the economics of immigration is a complex one about which a great deal has been written both in Australia and in other high-immigration countries. Due largely to data deficiencies, it is difficult to come to absolutely unambiguous conclusions about costs and benefits. Nevertheless, in an authoritative review published in 1990, Mark Wooden of the National Institute of Labour Studies concluded that of the three major Australian studies conducted up to 1988 (p. 17) using large-scale macro-economic models:

> Taken together, the three seem to suggest that immigration generally confers positive economic benefits on the Australian population, though it might be judged that the size of the measured effects is small.

More specifically, the review concluded that:

(i)   The evidence refutes the claim that immigration leads to increases in unemployment.

(ii)   If anything, the immigrant work force in the past has been more skilled than the domestic work force, and by implication more productive.

(iii) Immigrants have a strong tendency for home ownership which has been a major stimulant to the building industry.

(iv)   Given the tendency for rates of growth in GDP to understate the improvement in welfare of pre-immigration residents, there are scattered bits of evidence which lead us to be cautiously optimistic about the impact immigration has on living standards, though no study to date has been able to account for any adverse effects of congestion or negative environmental consequences.

Beyond the economic realm considerations of national security and international obligations have been highly influential in driving Australia's immigration program. National security was a particularly important concern after the Second World War when it seemed to many that Australia's claim to such a large agricultural, pastoral and mineral resource base could be readily challenged by our less developed but very populous neighbours to the north. Japan's territorial incursions into northern Australia during the war were fresh in people's minds. The threat of communism was also very worrying to many in the 1950s and 1960s and was embodied in the 'yellow peril' syndrome and the 'domino theory'. As late as the mid-1960s Australia's nearest northern neighbour, Indonesia, was threatened with a communist takeover.

4

National interests are also served by being regarded as a responsible global citizen. This is especially the case where refugees are concerned. Being a good global citizen is a matter of particular self interest in the contemporary period when Australia seeks to hitch a ride on the tailwind of the east and south-east Asian economic growth machine, as we have done since the 1980s. Our openness to immigration from Asian countries is regarded favourably by our trading partners. Their citizens are also conscious of such matters when they become tourists.

But while the economic and cultural benefits of multiculturalism have been extolled there has been considerable concern about the pace of cultural change within Australia. Many Australians regard the level of immigration as being too high, and are especially concerned about migration from non English-speaking nations. This stands in contrast to the view that multiculturalism is of value in its own right and will improve the nation's long-term economic prospects. While there are no objective means of resolving such differences they are politically significant and cannot be lightly disregarded.

The rhetoric and reality of globalisation

Referring back to the quotation from Sasskia Sassen with which this chapter opened, it is pertinent to expand on the notion of globalisation of which immigration is a key element. The human territorial units which comprise planet earth have been directly and indirectly linked in a multitude of interconnecting ways since time immemorial. In recent times, though, the density and forms of association have shifted dramatically. Trends over the past quarter century are often referred to under the rubric of 'globalisation', a buzz word covering so much as to be analytically useless but at the same time paradoxically pregnant with meaning. Key *economic* features of globalisation are the new international division of labour – notably exploitation in manufacturing of cheap labour in developing countries – massive growth in the scale and global reach of transnational corporations (TNCs) and shifting global trade flows reflecting differential patterns of regional economic growth. Integrated with these, themselves interconnected trends, are global flows of capital, information and people.

As far as Australia's current and longer term welfare is concerned most commentators would agree that economic development in east and south-east Asia holds the key. The national goal, supplemented by State-level initiatives, is to mesh with this growth engine. The flows linking Australia with Asia are manifold and mutually reinforcing. Although the categories overlap it is useful to think in terms of goods, services, people and information. These flows are grounded in various combinations and permutations in Australian cities and regions. Sydney has done especially well, or badly according to your perspective, in intercepting global investment and consumption flows and all that goes with them.

Cultural connections between actual or potential trading partners are also considered important. An example here is the symbiotic and dynamic relationship which is evolving between Hong Kong – a 'command and control centre' for corporations and a conduit of investment capital – and explosive economic growth based on manufacturing in the adjacent Pearl River Delta of China. There is a parallel relationship between the United States and Mexico. Less tightly symbiotic and not as strongly based on shared culture is the relationship between Australia and the Asian growth economies. Here discourses of multiculturalism, and the high numbers of Asian immigrants to Sydney in particular, are deployed by Federal and New South Wales State governments to stress cultural continuities. Australia's proximity to Asia relative to Europe and the United States is argued to give it an advantage in attracting business headquarters setting up to serve the Asia-Pacific region and tourists emerging from the Asian growth economies.

Integrally related to global flows of goods, capital and information are movements of people. Two forms – tourism and immigration – are especially important for Australia. Tourism, as is widely known, has become Australia's most important service export. In the 1980s numbers doubled from a base of about a million annually. The Australian Tourism Forecasting Council extrapolates a doubling of in-bound tourist expenditure from $6 billion currently to $15 billion by 2003. Alongside this explosive growth has been a marked shift in favour of Asian growth economies. In 1980, as a percentage of total tourists, Japan accounted for 5.4 per cent and the rest of Asia 9.9 per cent. The respective figures in 1990 were 21.7 per cent and 15.7 per cent. Of the capital cities Sydney attracts a quite disproportionate share of tourists. In 1991 30 per cent of international visitor nights were spent in Sydney, compared with 15 per cent in Melbourne and less than 10 per cent in each of Perth and Brisbane. Sydney's dominance is accounted for by Sydney airport's gateway function to Australia, together with the city's disproportionate share of internationally orientated business and immigrants, both of which generate tourism. Most important, however, is the fact that Sydney is really the only Australian city that has any sort of image in Asia.

Immigration to Sydney and Melbourne has always dominated other Australian cities. At the 1991 census, Sydney had 28.5 per cent and Melbourne 23.7 per cent of total overseas born persons. The figures for recent overseas born – those who settled between 1986 and 1991 – were 36.2 per cent and 23.5 per cent. Sydney has opened up a marked lead over Melbourne which, in the 1950s and 1960s, attracted marginally more immigrants than Sydney. The geographical source of immigrants to Australia, like other international links, has shifted markedly in favour of Asia. At the peak of the last immigration

6

boom, in the late 1980s, 42 per cent of immigrants were Asian whereas in the late 1960s only India ranked in the top ten of source countries and its position was tenth. The precise reasons for Sydney's capturing a disproportionate share of recent immigrants are uncertain but, apart from the influence of earlier settlers, which should favour Melbourne as much as Sydney, Sydney's greater integration with the global economy is clearly influential.

A study by Dwyer et al. (1993) found a clear relationship between immigration (the stock of persons born in other countries) and tourists visiting relatives in Australia from those countries. They argued that the changing centre of gravity of immigration sources from Europe to Asia can be expected to lead to more travel by immigrants from Asia and their relatives. It was not possible to measure any impacts of tourism on immigration; but it is possible that a relationship exists and that it is significant. Tourism is likely to increase demand for immigrant places and may result in greater numbers of skilled immigrants arriving.

A third type of people movement which has become economically important is education exports. Around 60,000 foreign students are now studying in Australia. Unlike tourism and immigration, however, foreign students are distributed more in proportion to population. Indeed Brisbane, Perth and Adelaide have shares of foreign students somewhat larger than their shares of national population.

Immigration, cities and regions

Embedded within the national-level debates and processes of globalisation discussed above, where immigrants choose to settle, across the cities, towns and rural regions of Australia, has been an important public issue, more especially in recent times. Comprehensive research completed under the auspices of the now defunct Australian government's Bureau of Immigration, Multicultural and Population Research (BIMPR) and its predecessors analysed the issues and reviewed statistics, literature and public debate as of the early 1990s (Murphy et al. 1990; Clarke et al. 1990; Fincher 1991).

Immigration has been, and continues to be, an important consideration in public discussion about the management of growth and change in Australian cities by State and Local government agencies. Debates have been especially pronounced in Sydney – the capital city of New South Wales and Australia's largest city. Because of its population (approaching 4 million) and its physical context, Sydney has the severest problems of air and water pollution and the least affordable housing in Australia. Perth, the capital of Western Australia, now also attracts a large share of immigrants but Perth is a much smaller city than Sydney and its environment is less pressured by human behaviour –

7

although there are concerns about the long term supply of water. In addition to these sorts of considerations, and this is the case in all Australian cities, governments at State and Local levels face increased difficulties in financing the provision and maintenance of urban infrastructure. Furthermore, at the level of Local government there have emerged contentious issues over 'ethno-specific' land uses such as places of worship.

As an outcome of Australia's forms of governance, issues have arisen that are qualitatively different to those observed in other parts of the world in relation to the effects of immigration on cities. In particular, relationships between Australian and State governments, and between State and Local governments, involve perpetual bargaining over shares of taxation revenue and other financial flows. Debate derives from the fact that, due to what is known as vertical fiscal imbalance, the Australian government 'controls the purse strings' while also managing the immigration program. It is, however, State and Local governments that are responsible for managing growth and change in the cities. Furthermore, Local government is in a weak position, being a creature of State legislation rather than the Australian Constitution. Moreover, it has a narrow revenue-base the augmentation of which can be controlled by State government. This is perhaps less of a problem than it is in some other countries because Local government in Australia provides a relatively narrow range of services. It is nevertheless an issue, especially in areas of lower than average incomes (Murphy and Watson 1994). At the level of Local government, so-called 'ethno-specific' services are marginal to the total task of government. In areas of lower income, where recent immigrants predominantly settle, coping with service demands deriving from immigration remains a significant task.

Social polarisation induced by economic restructuring has (since the 1970s) been a feature of Australian cities, as it has in cities elsewhere in the world (Murphy and Watson 1994). The residential location of recent immigrants, especially those who experience high levels of unemployment, is perceived by some as exacerbating polarisation and the social tensions which derive from it.

Managing growth and change in cities to achieve socially acceptable outcomes may benefit from considering cities as part of an 'urban system'. Thus in Australia there is a history – since the 1960s – of suggestions that the problems of the larger cities might be solved by actively encouraging people and businesses to live elsewhere. This was particularly the case in New South Wales and Victoria. There the urban growth problems of Sydney and Melbourne have been more pronounced than in smaller Australian cities. Various decentralisation (including growth centre) policies have been attempted. Another aspect of Australia's regional development has been the economic dominance of New South Wales and Victoria over the smaller States. Shifts in regional competitive advantage over the past quarter century have reduced this imbalance in favour of Queensland and Western Australia but other States have benefited less. From these considerations it has been argued that part of the solution to what are regarded as immigration-fuelled urban growth problems involves encouraging immigrants to settle outside of Sydney and Melbourne. This, it is suggested by proponents of the notion, would achieve the twin objectives of reducing growth pressures in the larger cities and increasing economic growth in the more peripheral State economies.

This book

Discourses on immigration played out in the popular media reflect the polarised positions of different interest groups. As noted above, the differing responsibilities and financial capacities of Federal, State and Local governments set the three levels at constant loggerheads with each other. Separate from this, although clearly a strong confounding influence on government, are interest groups including environmentalists, the so-called immigrant lobby, those concerned with social justice, those worried about the pace of cultural change engendered by immigration, and the simply far right wing, outright racist xenophobes. Debates about immigration's effects on the cities are integrally related to the differing agendas of these interest groups with the result that rational analysis, detached from polemical positions, is rarely on display. Attempts to disseminate rational analysis, particularly through the Federal government (in the last decade or so) have regularly been criticised by opponents of the scale and qualitative characteristics of the immigration program.

Accordingly, this book aims to present a concise and balanced review of the various urban outcomes and policy implications of Australia's immigration program. It recognises the interconnectedness of many of the issues and it also emphasises that points of debate about urban issues are sometimes really subsets of broader national considerations. While the book is obviously pre-occupied with the urban implications of immigration, since a proper consideration of these matters requires a good understanding of how cities 'work' the book may also be regarded as a review, of sorts, of contemporary Australian urban policy issues.

Chapters 2 and 3 review the location patterns of immigrants and the total population born overseas. In Chapter 2 the focus is on the national settlement system. It accounts for the contribution which immigrants have made over time to population growth in Australian cities. The chapter also addresses rates of household formation, since these are critical determinants of housing demand. As in Australia so much of new housing demand is expressed at low densities in raw new suburbs at the edges of the cities, the chapter also briefly reviews key features of Australian suburbanisation and the policy issues to which it has given rise. Chapter 3 considers patterns of immigrant settlement within the cities. The most important aspect of this chapter is its evaluation of the argument that high levels of residential concentration of some groups of recent immigrants, in association with pronounced social dislocation, and especially high levels of unemployment, have led to the formation of 'ghettos'.

Chapters 4, 5 and 6 turn to urban policy issues associated with immigration-driven population growth. Chapter 4 examines the implications for urban infrastructure provision of immigrant settlement patterns. To a very large degree demands for urban infrastructure deriving from immigrants are no different to those deriving from the Australian-born population. The public interest therefore relates to whether the managerial and financing capabilities of infrastructure suppliers are unduly tested by immigration-driven population growth and household formation. As was noted above, the fundamental question regarding the relationship between immigration and urban infrastructure concerns the funding responsibilities of the different tiers of government. Where immigrants settle – both between and within cities – is thus a crucial consideration for infrastructure planners. Chapter 5 reviews the effects of immigration on housing prices and affordability both between and within the cities. It also addresses the problems faced in particular by recent immigrants in obtaining access to appropriate and affordable housing. Chapter 6 presents information on urban environmental quality and considers the extent to which immigration-fuelled population growth contributes to the problem. As is the case with the question of urban infrastructure, it is argued that urban environmental quality has little to do with immigration as such. Because population levels and growth rates are implicated in declining environmental quality, immigration has however been a significant aspect of public debate. Like Chapter 4, this chapter is therefore a review of concepts and information pertinent to the debate rather than a review of research findings as such.

Chapter 7 examines relationships between immigration and urban labour markets. Among a range of considerations here are the high levels of unemployment experienced by some recent immigrants. In many cases the situation is exacerbated when immigrants settle in areas of cities which have poor access to jobs. Chapter 8 addresses the Australian regional development problem and its association with the choices made by immigrants as to which cities in which to live. In particular, the recent initiatives by the Australian government to encourage immigrants to live elsewhere than the largest cities is evaluated.

chapter two

Population growth, household formation and suburbanisation

Since the Second World War, more than 5.3 million immigrants have settled in Australia and some 1 million persons have emigrated, either Australia-born seeking a new life overseas, or immigrants and their Australia-born children returning home. Much of the net international net migration gain of 4.3 million persons has occurred in the two largest metropolitan areas of Sydney and Melbourne, and in the Western Australian capital of Perth, and in Adelaide and Brisbane to a significant but lesser extent. This chapter examines the contribution of immigration to the growth of the cities over the 50 years since the Second World War. It also examines the impact of other demographic elements – internal migration within Australia, fertility change, and increasing life expectancy – since each of these affects housing demand and the need for infrastructure and human services. An important theme of the chapter is suburbanisation and the factors which cause it, since the residential areas of Sydney and Melbourne occupy about 95 per cent of the built-up areas of these large metropolitan cities and in the other mainland State capitals residential areas occupy a slightly greater proportion of the land area of the cities. It is the lateral spread of the cities, their 'suburban sprawl', that has caused concern for many politicians and planners since the 1940s.

Before turning to the post-war period, growth trends between the turn of the century and the Second World War are summarised because it is important to consider the foundations on which post-war expansion took place. Both greater Sydney and Melbourne had achieved populations of 500,000 in 1900, with the population of Melbourne growing more rapidly than Sydney before the severe economic depression of the 1890s. On a national population base of little more than 4 million, Sydney and Melbourne in 1900 were larger in population size (and areal extent) than any European city at the time, with the exception of the very large imperial capitals, London, Paris, Vienna, Berlin, St Petersburg and Moscow. This population growth in Sydney and Melbourne was fuelled by strong immigration from the United Kingdom and by high population fertility; average completed family size was 6 to 7 children in both cities up to the early 1870s (Daly 1970). While steep fertility decline began after this date, average completed family size still exceeded four children in 1900. In sum, except for the depression years of the 1890s, annual growth rates of metropolitan Sydney and Melbourne averaged 3.5 to 4.5 per cent in the 1870s and 1880s and in the first decade of this century, virtually double the growth rates of the long economic boom after the Second World War.

Mention of the 1890s depression allows us to note a salient feature of Sydney's and Melbourne's growth: its boom and bust nature, particularly that of Sydney (Daly 1982). After the pause of the 1890s, British immigration and high but declining natural increase in the population recovered between 1900 and 1914 at which point global war interrupted immigration. Assisted immigration from Britain was restored in the more optimistic 1920s (Roe 1995). Foreign investment was also resumed since the costs of infrastructure to fund urban expansion were met by substantial overseas borrowing, the source of capital in the late 19th century and early years of this century being Great Britain. The Federal *Immigration Act* of 1901 and tight colonial legislation before it ensured that immigration from Asia including the Middle East would not occur or would be exceedingly limited. Even if the restriction acts had not been passed it is unlikely that the immigration intake in Australia would have been much greater because of its distance from the migration sources, Europe and China, and competition from the United States, Canada and some Latin American countries. By this time the agricultural and pastoral frontiers had been established and there was limited opportunity for British immigrants on the land. Immigration occurred more to the metropolitan cities. As a factor in urban population growth it compensated for the declining natural increase resulting from the fertility transition which ended with two-child families and lower marriage rates in the depression years of the early 1930s. Metropolitan growth slowed with limited natural increase and almost no immigration during the depression years but the suburban expansion resumed in the late 1930s, prior to its curtailment by the Second World War. This was made possible by a return to relatively full employment, better wages and the possession of a family motor car by the middle classes which made suburbanisation, which was less focussed on public transport, more possible.

By 1947 greater Sydney had 1.5 million people and greater Melbourne 1.3 million. Fifty years later in 1997, greater Sydney had 3.8 million people and greater Melbourne 3.5 million. It is to these developments, and the role of immigration, that we now turn.

Immigration, the long post-war economic boom and the cities

The shock of the Second World War and Australia's resultant vulnerability, along with the low population fertility of the 1920s and 1930s in Australia, resulted in a strong reassertion of the 'Populate or Perish' ethos after the Second World War. Australia, it was considered, needed more people for reasons of defence and labour force growth. A larger domestic population would provide better markets. Immigration on a large scale was regarded as necessary to solve these problems.

Initially the immigration target was set to produce a one per cent population increase per annum with a further one per cent through natural increase. This target was broadly achieved although immigration varied with economic fluctuations during the long 25-year economic boom, contracting around the period of the 'credit squeeze' in the early 1960s before expanding massively again in the late 1960s (Price 1970). While the overall demographic target – which had bipartisan political support – was achieved, it can hardly be said that the 'empty continent' was filled with people. This is because the immigration streams went primarily to the capital cities in south-eastern Australia, to Perth and to the secondary industrial cities of Wollongong and Geelong in the main, followed towards the end of the period by Newcastle. Immigration also contributed significantly to population growth in the Latrobe Valley urbanising region of Victoria (Zubrzycki 1964) and to the port and manufacturing centre of Whyalla (on the Spencer Gulf), the second city of South Australia. The capital city with the largest intake was Melbourne, followed by Sydney and then by Adelaide and Perth. This distribution, along with that of immigration to the secondary industrial cities, was influenced by the location of the expanding manufacturing base which was driven by Australia's post-war industrialisation policy. A major part of the immigration program in turn was aimed at obtaining labour for manufacturing industries, notably the early post-war Displaced Persons refugee intake and the Official Assistance Schemes which brought many British and northern Europeans, and some southern Europeans, to Australia. The role of manufacturing in Melbourne's post-war growth was particularly important and by the 1966 census manufacturing comprised 30 per cent of the work force in metropolitan Melbourne, the same proportion as in the industrial city of Newcastle in New South Wales. Many southern

European migrants, having found employment in Melbourne's manufacturing and building and construction industries, sponsored relatives to migrate via chain migration (what is currently called family reunion migration). Substantial Greek, Italian and Maltese communities evolved in Melbourne, although those in Sydney were also of considerable size and those in Adelaide and Perth were of consequence. Migrants from Britain, northern Europe and New Zealand were also important in the expansion of the service sector work forces of the southern mainland State capitals. In sum, 55 per cent of the total population growth in metropolitan Sydney between 1947 and 1971, and 59 per cent of that in metropolitan Melbourne, was directly due to immigration (Burnley 1974), compared to 42 per cent of national population growth (Table 2.1).

Several demographic features of growth in the metropolitan cities in this period have persisted into the contemporary era in Australia. First, the dominance of immigration as a component of population growth in Sydney and Melbourne. Second, the importance of internal migration in the growth of Brisbane, Perth and Canberra, most of which was the result of inter-metropolitan migration. Limited metropolitan growth has resulted from rural-urban migration in Australia, with the exception of migration from the Queensland hinterland to Brisbane (Burnley and Choi 1974; Bell 1992). Thirdly, there has been relatively limited international migration to Hobart and to Brisbane. The more limited, non-British immigration to Brisbane reflects the lesser expansion in manufacturing in Brisbane in the immediate post-war period and the fact that successive Queensland State governments were less interested in non-British immigration than the other State governments.

Major urban planning problems emerged in Sydney and Melbourne in the 1950s and 1960s period of rapid population growth, in part as the result of faulty assumptions used in the Cumberland Plan for metropolitan Sydney and the plan of the Melbourne and Metropolitan Board of Works (MMBW) in 1948 (Burnley 1974). Taking the case of Sydney, two key assumptions were in error. The first was the fertility prediction – which was too low – but the forecasters could not really be faulted for this since the consensus of opinion in the mid 1940s was that as the population had passed through demographic transition, the low fertility of the 1920s (at replacement level only) would continue. Indeed the large post-war immigration program had in part been predicated on this assumption. In reality the total fertility rate (average number of children per family) rose from 2.0 to 3.5 in the 1960s and the result was almost 300,000 more young people in metropolitan Sydney in 1972 than had been forecast in the Cumberland Plan. Forecasters could, however, have been more questioning about the immigration assumption used in their projections. It

Table 2.1 Components of metropolitan population growth in Australia, 1947-1966

Metropolitan division	Natural increase	Net migration of Australian-born	Net migration of overseas-born	Total population increase	Total annual per cent population increase
Numbers					
Sydney	378,784	266	463,413	842,463	
Melbourne	365,649	1,438	522,111	889,198	
Brisbane	123,672	87,720	108,820	320,212	
Adelaide	104,372	52,579	203,887	360,868	
Perth	103,910	37,455	114,488	255,853	
Hobart	28,746	9,946	18,286	56,978	
Per cent					
Sydney	45.0	0.0	55.0	100.0	2.3
Melbourne	41.1	0.2	58.7	100.0	2.4
Brisbane	38.6	27.4	34.0	100.0	2.9
Adelaide	28.9	14.6	56.5	100.0	2.5
Perth	40.6	14.6	44.8	100.0	3.1
Hobart	50.4	17.5	32.1	100.0	1.3

Note: (1) All boundaries adjusted to the 1966 boundary.
(2) The life table survival ratio was used to estimate net migration of the Australia-born; natural increase was calculated by using vital statistics; net migration of the overseas-born is therefore residual.

Sources: Australian Bureau of Statistics (various years: a).
Commonwealth of Australia (various years).

was not the volume of immigration that was in error but its relative location. It was assumed in New South Wales that immigrants would follow the regional distribution of the total population. In reality a disproportionate number settled in metropolitan Sydney relative to the balance of the State, a trend which has intensified in recent years (Burnley 1996a, Chapter 10). Immigrants settled in Sydney then as now because the jobs were there and because their communal networks and families were there. In the post-war period of full employment in Sydney, the labour market was tight in small towns and regional cities, and structural change meant declining work opportunities on the land. Agriculture was a capital intensive rather than a labour intensive industry. Thus there were approximately 300,000 more overseas-born in metropolitan Sydney in 1972 than had been forecast in 1947, and in sum almost 600,000 more people (2.7 million rather than 2.1 million). Such a magnitude of error resulted in major pressures on the planned green belt, housing shortages, and deficiencies in the numbers of schools and hospital beds. Similar problems resulting in part from forecasting errors occurred in metropolitan Melbourne.

This raises the issue of the need for accurate population forecasting for large urban regions in Australia. Had it been possible to forecast the population of metropolitan Sydney more accurately for the Cumberland Plan, then many of the contemporary and future planning problems could have been avoided. Thus it was not the substantial population growth and suburbanisation over a quarter century that was the problem but the lack of adequate knowledge about the extent, volume and nature of the population growth that was to take place. As mentioned, the unexpected rise in population fertility caught most analysts by surprise. Given that in most western industrialised countries the fertility decline beginning in the last quarter of the 19th century had bottomed out in the 1920s or 1930s to near replacement level (i.e. daughters replacing mothers without a surplus of births) it was rational to expect fertility to continue at this relatively low level. The Second World War had intervened and thus prolonged the low fertility trend in the United States, Australia, the United Kingdom, France and New Zealand. It was natural to assume that this low fertility would continue. Society had passed through the 'demographic transition' which had been codified as such by Thompson in 1929. With women obtaining secondary education and having entered the work force in increasing numbers following on the first feminist movement on the eve of the First World War, the average age at marriage had risen and the proportion married had also dropped from the late 19th century peak in Australia. It seemed that a new fertility and family regimen had come to stay. It is arguable, however, that the fertility decline in the second and third decades of this century was steepened by the First World War and its aftermath, and also by the sustained high general level of unemployment throughout the 1920s, well before the Wall Street crash of 1929 and the ensuing Great Depression of the 1930s. The return to more normal conditions after the Second World War resulted in an increase in fertility as the marriage rate rose. Whatever the case, the original demographic transition model proved a poor predictor of fertility trends in the period of the long economic boom between 1948 and 1972. More recent adaptations and expansions of the demographic transition model do allow for longer-run changes in fertility, bearing in mind that human attitudes towards family, children, and child bearing can change.

The other area of error in the post-war forecasts for Sydney and Melbourne was the level of immigration to the cities, and in particular the relative focus of immigration on these cities compared to other places. The focus on Sydney and Melbourne and also Adelaide and Perth reflected two processes: a greater immigration focus on these cities and less focus on Brisbane (and Queensland) and Hobart (and Tasmania), and a greater focus within the respective southern mainland States on the metropolitan capital cities than the balance of the States, with the exception of the cities of Wollongong, Geelong and Whyalla.

Furthermore, in the 1950s and 1960s there was considerable concern about decentralisation within the respective States, with New South Wales, Victoria and Western Australia actually having State government departments of decentralisation. The emphases of these agencies, however, was on regional development to slow rural-metropolitan population drift – internal migration to the cities – rather than to attract overseas immigrants to rural and regional centres. In fact rural-urban migration then, as now, was a minuscule factor, in relative terms, in population growth in Sydney and Melbourne, simply because the rural population bases were already so small compared with those of Sydney and Melbourne. Rural-urban migration was, however, of some importance in the growth of Brisbane, Perth and Hobart, in the post-war period. It was nevertheless assumed that more immigrants would settle in country areas and this was one reason why the large immigrant hostels through which many thousands of immigrants passed were located in Bathurst in the Central Western region of New South Wales and at Bonegilla in Victoria. At the time, unemployment levels were higher in rural areas and country towns than in the metropolitan cities, the agricultural and pastoral frontiers were at their maximum and there was a contraction under way in the number of farms and farmers due to technological changes and fluctuating commodity prices. The economic opportunities for immigrants in country areas were much more limited than in the metropolitan cities. Furthermore, expansion in manufacturing and building and construction employment occurred almost entirely in the metropolitan cities, and in the secondary industrial complexes of Wollongong, Geelong, the Latrobe Valley energy-resource towns of Victoria, and in Whyalla in South Australia. Finally, the country towns had no established ethnic communities to speak of whereas Sydney, Melbourne and Adelaide had small community nuclei of Italians, Greeks, Maltese, Lebanese and Polish, Russian and German Jewish people dating from the 1920s or earlier.

In addition, the formal demographic theories and models, as they existed then, did not accommodate the migration factor well. Even the more sophisticated cohort-component models which are used today by the demographic units in the various State government departments do not handle the migration components with ease. The migration components fluctuate in a way that fertility and mortality do not, in accordance with changing economic and political conditions, including the 'boom-bust' sequences alluded to earlier.

Immigration and the cities since the 1970s

Population growth rates in Australia after the early 1970s were significantly less than during the long post-war economic boom. The primary reasons were twofold: first, the sharp decline in population fertility in the 1970s and 1980s to below replacement level, and secondly, the overall lesser volume of immigration (despite two major immigration surges around 1979-1982 and 1987-1991). While immigration was substantial in specific periods, the much larger population base in Australia, and in Sydney and Melbourne, also meant that population growth rates on average were lower than hitherto: 1.0 to 1.4 per cent per annum in the 1980s and 1990s compared with 2.0 to 2.4 per cent in the 1950s and 1960s. However, in the immigration peak years 1987-1990 the annual rate of population growth in Australia was 1.8 per cent, the highest in the industrialised world.

Whereas the population growth rates of Sydney, Melbourne and Adelaide lessened considerably after the long post-war economic boom to annual rates of 1.1 to 1.4 per cent, those of Perth and Brisbane, although fluctuating, remained high between 2.0 and 3.4 per cent per annum over the 1971-1996 period. This reflected higher rates of economic growth in these cities and late expansion in manufacturing in contrast to Sydney, Melbourne and Adelaide where there were significant losses in manufacturing jobs due to industrial restructuring (Fagan and Webber 1994). There was significant economic growth in Brisbane and Perth in response to resource and pastoral developments in their large State hinterlands with multiplier effects in the manufacturing and tertiary sectors of the metropolitan economies and there was also rapid growth in their community service sectors. Migration became an important dynamic fuelling labour-force expansion in Brisbane and Perth but its components and overall impacts were considerably different from those in Sydney and Melbourne. In Brisbane internal migration, much of it interstate from Sydney and Melbourne, came to be more important than international migration whereas in Perth, international migration remained strong although internal migration was also important. In the 1947-1966 period, net internal migration had been of significance also in the growth of Brisbane and Perth, but not in Sydney and Melbourne as Table 2.1 shows.

Table 2.2 shows the components of population change in metropolitan Sydney in the fifteen years from 1986 to 1991 in five-yearly intercensal intervals. Estimated resident populations from each census 1976,1981,1986 and 1991 were used as the total population parameters; natural increase was calculated by use of intercensal vital statistics for the parameters; natural increase was calculated by use of intercensal vital statistics for the metropolitan statistical division (i.e. births-deaths) and net internal migration was calculated by use of the internal migration matrix tables from the 1981, 1986 and 1991 censuses (Bell 1992 and 1995a). These use the census and question about where people resided five years previously, and an adjustment was made for the 0 to 4 age group since those people who had moved with their parents were not alive five years previously. Net overseas migration was calculated as a residual. The 0 to 4 residence cohort of overseas-born counted at the 1981, 1986 and 1991 censuses was taken as the overseas-migration intake and this yielded a residual estimation of overseas emigration for the metropolis (Burnley 1996). Table 2.2 shows that net internal migration loss from Sydney has deflated the rate of population growth in Sydney that would have occurred from strong net overseas migration and natural increase. Indeed even during 1986-1991, when Sydney experienced the strongest five year immigrant gain in its history, the annual rate of population increase was below that of Australia as a whole. This was because metropolitan Sydney experienced a record net internal migration loss to Queensland, to Western Australia (Perth) and to the coastal zone of New South Wales. Much of the latter was associated with the 'population turnaround' or 'counterurbanistation' migration and settlement processes (Sant and Simons 1993; Hugo 1994a). A factor also deflating the direct impact of immigration on growth was emigration overseas which also ran at a relatively high level. This involved return migration of overseas-born persons and Australian-born emigration. Thus the dominant theme in Sydney and Melbourne (the latter also experiencing significant net internal migration losses) has been population turnover rather than massive rates of population increase.

Table 2.2   Estimated components in population change in metropolitan Sydney, 1976-1981, 1981-1986, 1986-1991

Period	Natural increase	Total net migration	Overseas immigration	Net internal migration	Estimated net overseas migration	Estimated emigration overseas	Total change	Average annual rate of change
1976-1981	115,200	20,600	148,160	−69,910	90,510	−57,700	135,800	0.85
1981-1986	121,960	71,200	150,070	−66,410	137,610	−12,460	193,150	1.15
1986-1991	132,030	69,260	246,970	−142,000	211,260	−35,710	201,290	1.13

Sources: Australian Bureau of Statistics (various years: b)
Australian Bureau of Statistics (various years: c)
Australian Bureau of Statistics (1983)
Australian Bureau of Statistics (1988)
Australian Bureau of Statistics (1993)
Bell (1992)
Commonwealth of Australia (various years)
NSW Department of Environment and Planning (1985)

Note: Internal migration matrix tables data have been adjusted for the 0-4 age group and for estimated under-enumeration.
The overseas immigration cohort has been adjusted to discount visitors.

The contrasting rates of population growth, and the variable components of population increase in the five mainland State capital cities, resulted in metropolitan Sydney having an estimated resident population of 3.75 million in June 1995, Melbourne 3.35 million, Adelaide 1.05 million, Perth 1.15 million and Brisbane–Moreton Bay 1.55 million. Whereas Adelaide was Australia's third largest metropolis at the end of the Second World War, it ranked fifth in 1995. The national capital, Canberra, also attracted strong internal migration, as Federal government functions were relocated to Canberra, and expanded in the post-war period and in the 1970s and early 1980s with private sector employment becoming more important there in the late 1980s. While internal migration was the strongest migration component throughout the post-war and 1970s periods, in the 1980s international migration became more important in Canberra. Hobart and Tasmania have attracted relatively few immigrants despite State government willingness to take more, and while Hobart experiences a net internal migration gain from rural areas of Tasmania, it experiences net internal migration losses to mainland Australia so that in consequence its rate of population growth has been relatively low.

Table 2.3 shows estimated net overseas migration and net internal migration in the States and territories of Australia in the two intercensal periods 1981-1986 and 1986-1991, as well as in the three years 1981-1984. In the case of New South Wales, Victoria, Queensland, Western Australia and South Australia, the trends shown are broadly indicative of those of the respective State capital cities. New South Wales, Victoria and South Australia had significant net internal migration losses, and it is interesting that the trend in South Australia was the reverse of what had occurred in the 1950s and 1960s. This trend in part accounts for the marked slowing of the population growth of Adelaide in recent years. Meanwhile there were strong net internal migration gains in Queensland, and while international migration was not insignificant there, it was less than that to Western Australia, even though the latter has little over half the total population of Queensland. In contrast to the post-war period, net overseas migration became more important than net internal migration in Canberra in the 1980s, although not in the early 1990s when immigration to Australia again declined due to recession. Overall migration in total has been more important relatively in Brisbane and Perth in recent years than in Sydney and Melbourne. In Brisbane, internal migration was the dominant migration component in growth whereas in Perth, international migration was dominant.

While population growth rates were less in Sydney and Melbourne, population increase in terms of numbers of people was quite notable. There were important quantitative impacts on the cities, particularly in Sydney, as the result of the changing direction of immigration, which is clearly evident in Table 2.3. Thus in 1981-1986, New South Wales absorbed 39.6 per cent of the overseas migration net gain in Australia; in 1986-1991 this share was

Table 2.3 Net estimated international migration by States and Territories of Australia, 1981-1994

	NSW	Victoria	Qld	South Australia	Western Australia	Tasmania	NT	ACT	Australia
Net international migration									
1981-86	168,022	112,126	48,500	28,319	54,464	3,859	4,758	4,519	424,567
1986-91	265,514	167,028	78,274	29,198	89,767	3,685	4,532	5,588	643,586
1991-94	66,892	37,689	17,628	6,569	19,372	364	1,471	−928	149,051
Net internal migration									
1981-1986	−68,822	−41,905	95,663	−8,384	17,198	−1,902	3,440	4,712	NA
1986-1991	114,027	−62,711	162,311	−4,145	17,088	377	7,040	8,150	NA
1991-1994	47,817	−81,468	141,047	−8,247	1,912	−4,058	−4,509	3,142	NA

Source: Australian Bureau of Statistics (1995)
Note: Year ending 30 June, 1994.

41.3 per cent, and in 1991-1994 it was 44.9 per cent. Within New South Wales, an increasing proportion of the overseas net migration gain occurred in metropolitan Sydney so that in the 1986-1991 period 37 per cent of the national overseas migration gain occurred in metropolitan Sydney while between 1991 and 1994 over 40 per cent of the overseas migration gain is estimated to have taken place in Sydney. For comparison, 20 per cent of the national population resides there.

Sub-demographic processes and metropolitan growth and change

Arguably, the rate of household formation and growth in new households is a more important parameter than rates of population growth in what has been happening to cities. This is because as new households form, a dwelling is required to be vacant for each new household either in established areas of the cities or on their fringes. These 'sub-demographic processes' underpin demand for housing. In the last 20 years, rates of household formation in Australia have been considerably above those of population growth and this has continued into the 1990s. The reasons for these higher rates have to do with the age structure of the population and associated population dynamics. First, the post-war baby boom cohorts are still passing through the family formation stage. Secondly, many people who migrated to Australia in the 1950s and 1960s had their children in Australia and these cohorts have also been entering the family formation age range. This is despite the decline in population fertility in the 1970s and 1980s that will not be felt in the family-forming age groups until the first decade of the twenty-first century. Thirdly, average household size has fallen over the past two decades for several reasons: declining fertility; young people leaving home to be independent; higher proportions of younger people not marrying but forming separate households; and more two-person and one-person households of older persons because of increasing life expectancy. Indeed, life expectancy in Australia has increased by almost eight years in the 27 years since 1970. Some 500,000 more people will be alive in Australia in the year 2001 than was forecast in long range projections in the early 1970s. Most of these people will be at older ages, due to a decline in mortality, particularly that from heart disease and stroke. And as elderly people normally live in one- or two-person households, over 300,000 dwellings will be taken up by the population which would not have survived had 1950s and 1960s age-specific mortality levels remained constant between 1970 and 2000. This means that younger populations which would have occupied this housing, much of which is in inner and middle ring residential districts of the metropolitan cities, have to occupy housing near the urban peripheries thereby increasing housing demand in these areas. The fourth reason for higher household formation rates is the impact of immigration itself. Immigration tends to be age selective and an appreciable proportion of immigrants tend to be at the family forming stage of the life cycle. While most immigrants do not buy directly into the new residential subdivisions on the edge of the city, they form new households on arrival, either owning or renting in established areas and this may increase demand in established areas and contribute to the suburbanisation of existing populations.

A fifth factor driving high growth rates in numbers of households has been the marked increase in divorce (and separation) rates, to over 35 per cent. Indeed the divorce rate after 30 years of marriage exceeds 40 per cent for some cohorts. Such persons set up separate homes, often in established areas of cities, and they make particular demands on sub-markets – for example the rental sector, or certain classes of owner-occupier dwellings, such as home units, lower cost townhouses and duplexes. This impact occurs because of the splitting of family assets associated with divorce, with at least one member of the previously married couple trading down in housing type and quality. Most of the single-parent families with children are accommodated in lower cost outer suburbs, or in public housing estates there, and in the inner city.

The importance of changing household size and rates of household formation higher than population growth can be illustrated in the case of Adelaide. The 1961 Adelaide plan projected high population growth, strong economic growth with full male employment, rising real incomes and the continuing expansion of urban areas to meet the population growth in which immigration and net internal migration gain were expected to feature prominently. In reality there was a marked decline in immigration to only 3.5 per cent of the national total in the 1980s and net internal migration losses as a result of restructuring in manufacturing and marked declines in employment in industrial sectors (Forster 1991; Hamnett and Parham 1992). However in the 1980s and early 1990s, the rate of growth in household formation was more than twice that of population growth in Adelaide. It is interesting that the 1962 Town Planning Committee predicted, with considerable accuracy, the amount of urban land required for the next 30 years. That land was indeed taken up, but by 300,000 fewer people than forecast. The rapid increase of households compared to population over the plan period was not foreseen (Metropolitan Adelaide 1992, p. 5). This also points to the continued consumption of space – in terms of a detached house on a piece of land with garden – on the part of a wide range of household types in the Adelaide situation. It is interesting also in this period that immigration from overseas to Adelaide was much less strong than hitherto and yet household formation and suburbanisation proceeded apace.

In Perth also, the rate of household formation has also been above that of population growth, but not to the same extent as in Adelaide (State Planning

Commission 1987). This is because the rate of population growth in Perth has been much greater than in Adelaide. The rate of household formation has actually been higher in Perth than in Adelaide, substantially due to migration; natural increase comprises only one-third of population growth (Metroplan 1990, p. 4), and overseas migration comprises two-thirds of all newcomers to Western Australia, 86 per cent of whom settle in metropolitan Perth.

The other sub-demographic process of importance in housing demand is the ageing of the population. This will be particularly important in Adelaide because of the age-selective internal out-migration in recent years (Hugo, Young and Rudd 1991) and the relatively limited immigration from overseas of younger people in the period since the late 1970s. It has been projected that by 2021 Adelaide's aged population (>65) will have doubled to around 250,000 people, which represents 23 per cent of the projected metropolitan population. As in Sydney, (NSW Government 1995, pp. 30-31) the proportion of elderly is likely to increase more rapidly in areas which currently have high levels of persons aged 45 to 64. In such areas this indicates the likely concentration of demand for smaller houses from older householders in the coming years. In Adelaide, one in four elderly people will be from non English-speaking backgrounds by 2021. In Sydney, the proportion will exceed a third. In sum, there are other key factors besides immigration which contribute to the expansion of cities and the need for new land for housing, and in consequence the demand for local services and infrastructure.

Immigration, metropolitan growth and suburbanisation

Immigration and suburbanisation

Australia was born urban and quickly grew suburban (Glynn 1971; Davison 1996, p. 2). In the 19th century, four ethoses strengthened the influence of the suburban ideal upon urban Australians (Davison 1987). The 'Evangelical' ethos called for a revival of homely virtues which could best be achieved in the suburbs where the suburban home would be a kind of temple in which the wife ruled as 'Angel of the Home' (Davidoff and Hall 1987). The 'Romanticist' ideal envisaged the careworn city man repairing his 'battered spirits through communion with the beauties of nature', via a 'suburban residence with a small portion of land attached' (Loudon 1982, p. 8). This could be achieved even with terrace housing. The house garden was an important feature of the suburb, and it contributed to more space being required for urbanisation and suburbanisation. The 'Sanitarianist' ideal promoted 19th century suburbanisation because of the warnings which doctors and sanitary engineers were promulgating about the deadly pollution of the cities and particularly that of the slums. Suburbs were promoted for their safety. The fourth ethos which reinforced suburbanisation was that of capitalism, particularly the imperative to consume. Indeed the economic historian Butlin (1965) has shown how important the building and construction sector was in the economies of Sydney and Melbourne in the 19th century, much of which was associated with the construction of suburban housing and infrastructure. Of course technology, including the railway, the horse-drawn tram, and later the steam and electric trams made 19th and early 20th century suburbanisation possible, along with sewerage reticulation and the septic tank.

There were several other reasons why the suburbs flourished so well in 19th and early 20th century Australian cities. First, the suburban ideal arrived with the nation's European colonists, and it was strongly promoted by the state in the colonial period. Secondly, it was attractive to immigrants who themselves had left the crowded and often poverty-stricken cities of industrialising Britain. Many who could not obtain land, space and independence in the more densely populated cities of the homeland aspired to achieve these things in suburban Australia. To a certain extent, these factors were influential with British immigrants to Australia in the post Second World War period (Richardson 1974). Australia's suburbs in the 19th and early 20th century were shaped, decisively, by the successive waves of English, Irish, Scots and Welsh immigrants who pioneered them.

The demand for land, for space and for independence have always been prominent in the aspirations of immigrants to Australia (Davison 1993, p. 7). This has been long recognised in terms of rural settlement and the agricultural and pastoral frontiers: yet in volume of people it was more important in terms of the then *suburban* frontiers. Many remembered the experience of living as urban and rural tenants, and had longed to be free of the landlord and bailiff. It was not only British immigrants who longed for homes of their own. In post Second World War Australia, immigrants from peasant backgrounds in eastern and southern Europe often acquired their own inner and outer city suburban homes more rapidly even than the Australian-born (Australian Population and Immigration Council 1973, p. 9; Burnley 1972). It was home ownership, rather than space or privacy, that the southern European immigrants wanted to obtain. To achieve home ownership, they often were ready to sacrifice some of their personal space and family privacy that British immigrants regarded as being most important (Burnley 1973). This sacrifice for home ownership on the part of the southern Europeans was achieved in the inner suburbs of Sydney, Melbourne, Adelaide and Perth in the first instance. We return to this phenomenon and its impact on city form and structure in Chapter 3.

A third reason why the suburbs proliferated in the late 19th and early 20th centuries was that suburban residents were able to take advantage of relatively high wages, low unemployment, low-cost land and developing public transport services, notably the railway, omnibuses and trams. Indeed, Sydney and Melbourne at the time were star shaped, with suburban residential developments extended along the public transport routes. A fourth reason was that suburbanisation was promoted by Australia's system of strong central government and relatively weak Local government. By central government we mean the respective colonial and later State governments; by Local government we mean municipal and shire governments. At this time, Local government was even more fragmented than is currently the case. The colonial governments and their State successors took on many of the costs of suburbanisation which would otherwise have had to have been carried by the local community (Davison 1993, p. 6). These costs included those of new schools, main roads, police stations, sewerage, suburban railways and other infrastructure. Thus, at an early date, Australians were subsidising suburban growth from their public (colonial and later State) treasuries. Furthermore colonial administrators were determined to avoid reproducing the grim conditions of large sections of British and continental European cities, although some poverty-stricken slums developed, such as in the Rocks and parts of Surry Hills in Sydney (Kelly 1986).

Some have argued that a pattern of over-consumption of space was associated with Australian urbanisation and that this has continued to the present, therefore compounding the planning, economic and social problems of Australia's large cities. It is interesting, now, that when Donald Horne designated Australia as being 'the lucky country' he referred to its status as 'the first suburban nation', a fact first established by Adna Weber in 1900 in a study of comparative urbanisation. The high average incomes enjoyed by Australian workers during the late 19th and early 20th centuries contributed strongly to the growth of the suburbs (Butlin 1965, p. 8). Low-cost land which could be easily serviced, low-cost building materials, cheap methods of building construction and the ready availability of housing finance enabled people in Australia to buy or rent more land and house for their wages than equivalent persons in the United Kingdom or the United States (Frost 1991, pp. 113-117).

It is also arguable that the early suburbanisation, to which immigration contributed demographically, was a relatively democratic form of suburban-isation (Davison 1993, p. 9). The word 'democratic' here is used in an equality sense, and relative equality between suburbs in the late 19th and early 20th centuries existed. A related aspect of this more 'democratic' form of suburbanisation was that Australia's suburbs have relied more heavily than in the United States, Britain or Canada, on the support of the state, as noted above. The state supplied new schools, police stations, suburban railways and other infrastructure, costs which were borne by the local community or private developers elsewhere through locally based taxation assessed on landed property, as in North America. In Australia, sales of Crown lands and customs duties administered by the state paid for these expenses. The impact of this was that the development costs faced by ratepayers were lower in the new suburbs.

27

State funds guaranteed a relatively common standard of state schooling and public service across all suburbs and thus reduced one of the main motives for class differentiation between them. It may be that class differentiation is now increasing, for in Sydney at the present time there is a much higher proportion of public schools overall but in the eastern suburbs and upper north shore, over 50 per cent of students today attend private schools. In the late 19th century, however, Australian suburbanites placed less value on social exclusiveness than American and British suburbanites (Morris 1889, p. 58; Trollope et al. 1873) and there was almost certainly a greater social mix in Australian suburban neighbourhoods, as indicated by house types at least, than in American and British cities (Fricker 1978; Zunz 1982). Home ownership was a key factor, as now, in moving to the then urban fringe. A reason why colonial governments favoured home ownership was that with a nation, and cities, of small property owners, there would be less chance of social revolution because individuals would have a stake in the existing system. The owner-occupied house standing on its own ground was not only a way of obtaining a small property, and thus providing for one's old age, but it was also the source of economic, social and psychological benefits not found in a rented terrace or room in the inner city. In 1900, for example, almost 90 per cent of the terrace housing in inner city Sydney was rented even though over 50 per cent of the housing in the metropolitan area of 500,000 persons was inhabited on an owner-buyer basis.

In sum, many of the aspirations, values and political circumstances giving rise to the great geographical spread of Australian metropolitan cities were established by the turn of the century. In the 20th century, however, and especially in the half century since the Second World War, the connection between living standards, values and suburbanisation has become more complex. During the last 50 years, Australia's lead as 'the first suburban nation' has been ended by other lands, and as gentrification of various types has created alternative styles and standards of urban prosperity (Davison 1993, p. 8; Kendig 1979).

Today, Australians are witnessing the most significant challenge to their urban, and particularly their suburban way of life in more than a century. This challenge is posed by the relative decline of those conditions of economic prosperity and benign technological development which we have experienced during the last 150 years or so (Davison 1996, p. 1). Economic scarcity and the threat of environmental catastrophe have made suburban sprawl seem as wasteful and environmentally negative as it once seemed socially and environmentally safe. The reaction to the suburban way of life is partly because it is less affordable (in total cost including infrastructure and human services) but also because the social arrangements and goals, and political structures that supported this way of life, are now being questioned. Declining immigration and changing sources of immigrants, declining fertility and smaller government have produced a new urban agenda in which urban consolidation is argued to be both more economical and more attractive (Davison 1996, p. 2). However, while many politicians and some urban planners support consolidation to slow the geographic expansion of cities and thus facilitate the provision of infrastructure and human services, several urban analysts are strongly critical of the urban consolidation thrust, most notably Troy (1996).

Immigration and suburbanisation since the 1940s

Unquestionably immigration had a substantial impact on Sydney, Melbourne, Adelaide and Perth between 1947 and 1971, and has had a major impact on Sydney, Melbourne, Perth and Canberra in the 25 years since 1971. The impacts were on population growth, household formation and population structure: directly, through the presence and contribution of immigrants and indirectly in the impact of their Australia-born children. These direct and indirect impacts have been felt more in some areas within the metropolitan cities than others, and have variously affected demand for human services such as schools and hospitals and also the need for specific services to overcome language difficulties, particularly in Sydney. Not only has the proportion of persons of non English-speaking origin in the Australian immigration intake increased markedly in recent years but that share has been even greater in Sydney (Burnley 1996a): between 1987 and 1996, 40 per cent of immigrants to Australia have settled in metropolitan Sydney and in the same period 44 per cent of non English-speaking background immigrants settled there. The other metropolitan city in recent years in which total immigration and that from other countries speaking a language other than English was disproportionate, relative to city size, was Perth. The metropolitan cities in which overall immigration and settlement of persons from countries speaking a language other than English have been low in recent years are Adelaide and Hobart. Apart from the secondary industrial cities in New South Wales, and some regional cities, relatively few immigrants have settled in non-metropolitan towns and rural areas, especially in recent times. Where such settlement has continued, it is mostly the result of small-scale, long-term chain migration.

Historically, immigration from most countries of continental Europe involved the replacement of local households in established, inner city areas although many settlers from Britain, the Netherlands and New Zealand settled directly in outer suburbia. But as most settled in established areas, the impact of immigration on population growth in the outermost ring of suburbs was less than in the metropolitan cities as a whole (Burnley 1972, 1974). The inner and middle ring settlement presence reflected the earlier location of cheaper housing and also local cohesiveness of established ethnic communities and kin. Thus in the period 1947-1971, whereas immigration directly contributed 55 and 58 per cent respectively of population growth in metropolitan Sydney and

Melbourne it accounted for only 25 per cent of growth in the outer suburban ring of Local Government Areas in both cities.

A higher proportion of recent immigration has gone to both higher and lower income outer suburbs and newer release areas than hitherto, although appreciable numbers have settled in established areas. Thus between 1976 and 1991 immigration directly contributed 32 and 37 per cent respectively of population growth in the outer rings of Local Government Areas of Sydney and Melbourne, compared to a quarter of the growth in the period of the long economic boom post-war. While, however, the relative impact on the outer suburbs was greater than in the 1950s and 1960s, it was still significantly less than the impact of immigration on the growth of the metropolitan cities as a whole in this later period: 65 and 82 per cent in Melbourne and Sydney respectively. It must be remembered, however, that Sydney's and Melbourne's total population growth rates during this time were deflated considerably because of net internal migration loss rates to other parts of Australia particularly in the case of Sydney (Table 2.2). The demographic impact of immigration was thus magnified considerably. Furthermore, birth rates had declined so that natural increase had fallen and, in addition, net internal migration losses from most outer suburban areas to other parts of Australia also took place, thus increasing the immigrant share in outer suburban population growth (Burnley and Murphy 1994). Even so, natural increase and intra-urban migration together were responsible for most outer suburban population growth in Sydney and Melbourne in the later period (Burnley 1996). The intra-urban migration reflects the net impact of movers, mostly young adults, from the inner and middle ring areas of the respective cities who have moved out to purchase their first home and start their families (Burnley, Murphy and Jenner 1997). Housing demand in the outer suburbs is also strong as the result of 'in situ' household and family formation as individuals leave homes which were first settled by their parents 20 to 30 years earlier during the long economic boom and need to rent or buy other housing on or near the periphery of the cities. In other words, local household formation in outer suburbia generates a demand for new housing quite apart from migration of any kind.

Proportionately fewer immigrants have settled in the inner suburbs, in recent years, for several reasons. First, the cost of housing has increased markedly in the inner city (especially in Sydney) relative to much of the metropolitan periphery, in part due to gentrification in the inner city (Kendig 1979). Secondly, most of the lesser cost housing and lower income districts are now near the distant edges of the metropolitan areas. Thus whereas the lower income and poorer housing districts in the years soon after the Second World War were in the inner city close to the central business districts of Sydney and Melbourne, the situation had largely changed by the 1990s with lower income districts in certain outer peripheral areas. Thus a fundamental difference has emerged in the location of lower cost housing and poorer populations between Australian and American cities (Murphy and Watson 1993). In the latter, the poorer areas on the whole are still in the inner city. In Sydney and Melbourne, with certain exceptions, less affluent immigrants are less able to afford to settle in the inner city than hitherto. Thirdly, many skilled, professional and business migrants have settled in outer, higher income areas, as in Sydney's upper north shore. Fourthly, lower income immigrants, particularly refugees from Asia and Latin America, have settled in strength in outer, lower cost housing areas, as in Sydney's Fairfield and Liverpool, and Melbourne's Springvale Local Government Areas. Many of these outer, lower income areas are close to, or contain the migrant reception centres, which have been a factor in the localisation of immigrant settlement (Whitelaw 1980; Wilson 1989; Burnley 1989).

Despite these changes, it is evident that an important trend which occurred in the post-war period within the cities has continued into the present, notably in Sydney. This is the 'replacement' function of immigration, whereby immigrants replace a suburbanising population which is vacating inner and middle ring areas. Table 2.4 shows correlations between overseas in-migration rates by Statistical Local Areas (SLAs) in Sydney and intra-urban out-migration rates, and internal out-migration rates. It is clear that many immigrants were settling in inner and middle ring areas from which higher rates of out-migration were occurring to other parts of Sydney, especially between 1976-1981 and 1986-1991. On the other hand, the associations with internal migration rates (moves out of Sydney to other regions of Australia) were negative in the 1980s. The highest rates of internal migration loss were in the outer suburbs where fewer immigrants settled. The highest intra-urban out-migration rates were in the inner and older middle ring areas, where more immigrants settled.

It is clear then that several other factors are contributing to the spatial expansion of the metropolitan cities, bearing in mind that immigration interrelates with some of these. First is the high rate of household formation, which results in strong demand for new detached housing on the metropolitan periphery or in infill areas where these exist. Secondly, there is the prevailing preference of the majority of households, immigrant and Australian alike, for detached housing for child raising and for general living. There is no evidence that this strong preference has lessened for the population as a whole. Given the cost of housing in inner city areas, and in the case of Sydney and Melbourne higher rents and prices near the beaches and waterways, many young couples have no option but to purchase a dwelling either some distance from the city centre in an established area, or in new release areas on the metropolitan fringe. It will be remembered from the earlier discussion that a strong ethos of the value of suburban location and lifestyle was established in the 19th century by British immigrants and locals, and was reinforced by planners' and idealists' visions of optimal neighbourhoods and garden suburbs. Many immigrants have also been captivated by the suburban ideal. If Australia was the first suburban nation, suburban environments developed apace in the United States and

Britain, and north-west Europe, and via models purveyed by television and film on an international scale. These 'ideal type' symbols of success have thus been normalised globally. The suburbanisation thrust, with its associated low population densities, has remained a common goal for immigrants and Australians who value a family-centred lifestyle. Furthermore, immigrants tend to avoid higher density developments in the long term, although some recent arrivals, particularly refugees in western Sydney, have settled in medium density developments on an interim basis.

Conclusion

Immigration has unquestionably been a dominant component of population growth in Sydney, Melbourne and Perth, and an important component in the growth of Brisbane and Adelaide. This is especially the case when the children born to immigrants in Australia are included. Immigration has also contributed to suburbanisation, more so in recent years, although its share of suburban population growth has been less, at least in Sydney, Melbourne and Perth, than in metropolitan populations as a whole. A factor in this has been the replacement aspect of immigrants occupying housing vacated by the native-born, in inner and middle ring SLAs. The impact on outer suburban SLAs has been uneven, ranging from disproportionate, in the case of the cosmopolitan Fairfield and Springvale SLAs in outer Sydney and Melbourne respectively, to minimal as in the case of Gosford and Wyong in outer northern Sydney, and Sandringham and Brighton SLAs in outer south-eastern Melbourne. In the first 25 years post-war, the major problem for the cities themselves was not the large-scale immigration but the difficulties of medium and long term population and housing demand forecasts, and thus the necessity of reactive planning and management responses to an unfolding situation. In the last 25 years, the problems have become more complex, because of changing demographic structures and an increasing plurality of household forms, due to demographic ageing, divorce and remarriage, declining fertility, and the greater social acceptance of persons living alone. The population, household size and dwelling relationships have altered as average household sizes have fallen. A problem now, although it is only a problem in a relative sense, is that the smaller households are often consuming as much urban space as the larger households previously.

Where immigrants live

By 1991 there were 1.05 million overseas-born in metropolitan Sydney who comprised 30 per cent of the metropolitan population. The overseas-born population in metropolitan Perth comprised over 33 per cent of the metropolitan population of 1.1 million. Including the Australian-born populations with overseas-born parents, first and second generation populations together comprised 54 per cent of the total population of Sydney, 58 per cent of the population of metropolitan Perth, and 51 per cent of the population of metropolitan Melbourne. The direct impact of overseas immigration on Brisbane, Adelaide and Hobart has, however, been less in the last 20 years than in the 1950s and 1960s. Moreover significant internal migration of the overseas-born has been taking place from New South Wales and Victoria to Brisbane and Canberra (Bell and Cooper 1995). It is to be expected that, overall, the impact of immigration within the cities on the population structure, small business and community relations in local areas has been profound and this has indeed been the case (Burnley 1994).

Extent and significance of ethnic concentration

Of concern to some people is the level of ethnic concentration or segregation in cities. This concern may be prejudicial; it may be associated with the notion that if there is residential segmentation then there cannot be 'one Australia', or that if there is strong concentration or segregation, then inequality may result with structural disadvantage (Marcuse 1996). A further concern is that some immigrant groups may make disproportionate demands on local social services (Birrell 1993, p. 30).

A commonly used indicator of residential concentration is the index of dissimilarity. This has been widely used in Australian studies since the early works of Burnley (1972) and Stimson (1970), and has been used by Hugo in the *Atlases of the Australian People* based on the 1986 census, and in the new series based on the 1991 census (Hugo and Maher 1995; Beer and Cutler 1995; Burnley 1996; Hugo 1996; Jackson 1996). The index is the per cent of a given birthplace group that would have to redistribute itself by spatial categories to have the same distribution as the standard population – in this case the Australian-born population. In Table 3.1 indexes of dissimilarity are shown for a range of birthplace groups in four metropolitan cities of different size in Australia at the 1991 census. In considering the table there are some cautionary comments. The index is sensitive to the number of spatial units, in this case, the Statistical Local Areas (SLAs) that are employed (Woods 1976). In the largest city, Sydney, there were 43 SLAs, in Adelaide 30, in Perth 26, and in the smallest city, Canberra, there were 100. Hence the SLAs were much larger in population size and area in Sydney than in Canberra. In general, the more spatial units there are, the higher the index values are likely to be. Thus it might be expected that the indexes would trend higher in Canberra. In fact, this mostly did not occur.

In general it can be said that groups with index values below 20 are lightly concentrated or relatively dispersed; values between 20 and 50 suggest moderate concentration; those between 50 and 80 imply strong concentration and those with index values over 80 are segregated to a large degree. This categorisation summarises a range of categorisations in the international literature (Lieberson 1963; Winship 1977; Hugo 1992; Beer and Cutler 1995; Peach 1996). Turning to Table 3.1 it is clear that no group could be classed as 'segregated' in any of the four cities, and that only a small number were 'strongly concentrated' as defined: in Sydney, those born in Vietnam or Lebanon, which is partly a function of the recency of arrival in Australia of these communities (mostly since 1975). In Adelaide only those born in Vietnam could be viewed as being strongly concentrated, whereas in Canberra, those born in Turkey and Egypt could be seen as strongly concentrated, bearing in mind the larger number of spatial units used in the Canberra case. In Perth, no groups were strongly concentrated using the criteria stated above. Furthermore, with the exception of the Vietnam-born the Asia-born groups were not more residentially concentrated than the groups born in continental Europe even although the former were more recent arrivals in Australia than the latter.

It is arguable that the conditions for segregation or strong concentration are less critical in Australian cities than in American or European cities (Murphy and Watson 1993). It is, however, clear that high unemployment did occur in areas of Vietnamese, Arabic, and Spanish-speaking residential concentration in western Sydney (Burnley and Forrest 1995). In part this is because of the

Table 3.1 **Indexes of dissimilarity of birthplace groups in Sydney, Adelaide, Canberra and Perth, 1991**

Birthplace	Metropolitan area			
	Sydney	Adelaide	Canberra	Perth
UK and Ireland	11.9	20.1	6.4	13.3
Germany	12.9	7.9	14.0	8.1
Greece	49.7	33.8	30.4	44.3
Italy	35.6	37.3	21.8	32.5
Netherlands	15.8	16.5	17.7	12.6
New Zealand	20.9	11.7	13.4	8.8
Poland	31.0	25.2	24.5	23.7
Former Yugoslavia	37.3	26.9	21.5	37.0
Vietnam	67.1	53.0	33.1	48.1
India	23.2	13.9	20.1	20.5
Lebanon	52.2	19.7	41.8	25.2
Malaysia	29.5	33.2	21.3	30.2
Malta	39.8	24.1	31.3	21.2
South Africa	28.1	23.0	25.9	10.9
USA	36.1	24.7	23.7	17.7
China	43.6	26.4	31.1	31.7
Egypt	31.2	19.5	55.0	21.4
Philippines	35.8	20.8	26.8	16.2
Hong Kong	40.4	34.4	30.5	31.2
Chile	42.5	36.2	n.a.	29.6
Singapore	36.2	28.9	n.a.	27.7
Spain	36.9	16.5	37.6	19.9
Turkey	48.9	33.8	59.2	36.4
Former USSR	35.3	28.3	29.3	26.5

Source: Beer and Cutler, (1995); Hugo (1996)

disadvantage inherent in having a limited command of English and recency of arrival, but it is also through job losses in manufacturing industry due to industrial restructuring. These issues are discussed later in this chapter and, in a different context, in Chapter 7. There is some evidence that movement of Vietnam-born persons into the concentration areas from elsewhere in Australia has taken place over time, possibly to obtain communal support in a situation of economic adversity (Burnley 1996b; Birrell 1993).

Thus while there are strong ethnic concentrations in some areas of Australian cities, such concentrations are not totally segregated enclaves. Yet some, because of their size and the social visibility of their inhabitants, continue to attract critical attention. Birrell (1993) for example states:

> that to the extent Indochinese concentrations challenge Australian views about the impact of immigration it is more out of concern that 'Asian' enclaves symbolise a new Australia marked by separate and 'visible minorities'.

This has in essence been the view of the eminent critic of Australia's more recent ethnically diverse migration and settlement (Blainey 1993).

One of the strongest academic critics of ethnic concentration formation in Australian cities in recent times has been R. Birrell. Focussing on the Vietnamese, in part because of the size of this population in Australia, Birrell has argued that in the Fairfield (Cabramatta) area of outer western Sydney and the Springvale area of outer eastern Melbourne, ethnic ghettos have begun to form (Birrell 1993). He defines 'ghetto' in terms of the level of ethnic residential concentration occurring in a given area and the association of socioeconomic disadvantages with the ethnic concentration. He argues that while in the post-war period, levels of residential concentration of some southern-European-born groups were virtually comparable with those of the Vietnam-born today, the levels of socioeconomic disadvantage associated with such concentrations were far less than in the case of the Vietnamese today. While this is partly true, it has in fact been shown that in the late 1970s levels of unemployment and relative poverty reached 20 per cent among recent arrivals in Italian settlement areas in Leichhardt in inner Sydney and Bossley Park (Fairfield) in the outer suburbs, among Lebanese in Lakemba, and among persons from Greece and the former Yugoslavia in Marrickville and Newtown in the inner city (Burnley 1985).

Jupp (1990, vol. 2, p. 47) defines ghettos as 'districts of multiple social problems inhabited primarily by a distinct ethnic group or groups generally held in low esteem by the majority population living elsewhere'. Jupp does not consider that the Vietnamese concentrations in Cabramatta (Sydney) or in Footscray or Springvale (Melbourne) are ghettos as he has defined them. He argues that these aggregations are occurring in areas already marked by diverse ethnic populations, to which the Vietnamese-born (who comprise both ethnic Vietnamese and ethnic Chinese) are mostly adding another 'layer'. He argues that the impression visitors get of high Asian concentrations, as in the Cabramatta area of Fairfield in Sydney, reflects the zone's development as a 'focal point' for ethno-specific institutions. It thus draws in a large number of ethnic group members from surrounding municipalities for shopping, business and social relations associated with institutions. Jupp has also been impressed by Cabramatta's commercial vibrancy and its potential for tourism (Jupp 1990, vol. 1, p. 130). In a later reply to a critique by Birrell of the Jupp, McRobbie and York (1990) monograph on ethnic concentrations in Australian cities, Jupp (1993, p. 51) stated that fieldwork undertaken by his team suggested that:

> far from being a deprived area, the commercial rents and purchase prices in Cabramatta were so high that many new arrivals cannot enter the booming commercial sector. Fairfield City Council enjoys a strong rate base resulting from the development of John Street from a once sleazy and nondescript shopping strip to a major regional shopping centre.

Birrell (1993) on the other hand argued that there was high unemployment and low educational achievement in Cabramatta. Jupp (1993, p. 51) agreed that this may be so although he considered that Birrell did not make valid comparisons. It is certainly true that high unemployment was associated with first and second generation persons born in Vietnam who were resident in Fairfield SLA in 1991 (Burnley 1995), bearing in mind that several other immigrant groups living in Fairfield also have high unemployment levels. Birrell's assertions concerning low educational achievement in the areas of residential concentration in Fairfield are less evident. Indeed, while high unemployment was evident among second generation and some young first generation persons born in Vietnam in Fairfield and Liverpool in western Sydney in 1991, the work force participation ratios in these age groups were low. This in turn implied that educational participation levels were high, as indeed they were.

Jupp (1993, p. 52) argued that many non-Indochinese areas in western Sydney and Melbourne, such as Green Valley, Liverpool, Campbelltown, Mt Druitt, Broadmeadows or St Albans evidence comparable or even worse social situations, often affecting native-born Anglo-Australians. Thus to Jupp, the important factor was not Indochinese concentration but the crisis of the former 'greenfield' industrial regions of the major cities. While Jupp (1993, p. 52) argued that ghetto conditions did not occur with any of the immigrant ethnic groups so far documented, he did consider that ghetto conditions could arise in areas settled by refugees in public housing (Jupp 1990, pp. 76-78), such as in public housing concentrations at North Richmond in Melbourne.

Overall, the experience of major immigrant ethnic concentrations in Australian cities has been found to be qualitatively different from that in American and European cities (Jupp 1993, p. 52; Viviani and Coughlan 1993). There are though serious social issues in these concentrations and similar areas but the ethnic composition of disadvantaged communities is not the central issue. Viviani and Coughlan (1993) also argue that we need to have socioeconomic, birthplace and language data at a small geographical scale over time (at least 10 to 15 years) and more information as to relative social disadvantage in these areas before we can come to a conclusion that the characteristics of a ghetto as defined by Jupp et al. (1990) are developing. In a recent publication Viviani (1996) states that the Cabramatta concentration of Chinese from Vietnam and ethnic Vietnamese is not a ghetto because there is much residential mobility into and out of the locality, on the part of persons of Vietnamese and other origins. And in an earlier study, Wilson (1990) showed through a careful questionnaire survey of Vietnamese families in western Sydney that a gradual process of residential dispersion was occurring and that an appreciable proportion of the residentially concentrated group intended to move out in time.

However, a study conducted at the SLA scale, giving estimates of net internal migration, found a process of net in-migration of Vietnam-born from other parts of Sydney (and almost certainly Australia) to the Fairfield SLA which contains the Cabramatta locality (Burnley 1996a). A study in progress by C. Maher using the internal migration matrix tables from the 1991 census confirms this finding. These tables use the question 'Where did you reside five years previously?' and are cross-tabulated by birthplace. While there were Vietnam-born outflows from SLAs of strongest relative concentration, the inflows of Vietnam-born from other parts of Sydney to Fairfield SLA, and from other parts of metropolitan Melbourne to Springvale and adjacent areas during 1986-1991, were stronger than the outflows. A similar trend has been observed in a detailed sample survey of Cambodian settlers who also formed a strong concentration in the Fairfield area of western Sydney (Melville 1995). Such net internal migration to a concentration area does not in itself cause any problems for the wider society and is only of concern if it results in less equality of opportunity or an increase in socioeconomic disadvantage for the immigrant group itself. The issue of whether there is significant socioeconomic disadvantage associated with ethnic concentrations is discussed below.

Before consideration of the socioeconomic characteristics of concentrations, some further definitions of 'ghettos' are discussed with reference to the Australian situation. Eyles in the *Dictionary of Human Geography* (Johnson et al. 1994), follows one of Ward's (1982, p. 158) definitions of ghetto as a 'residential district which is almost exclusively the preserve of one ethnic or cultural group'. For a group to be 'ghettoised', most members of the group are found in such areas. Peach (1996, p. 216) considers that this dual definition is required for the delimitation of a ghetto. He found that no such ghettos were identifiable in any British city despite the migration of more than 3 million persons from the 'new' Commonwealth countries. Peach (1996, p. 217) has distinguished between what might be called 'reputational' ghettos such as the Irish, Polish, German and Italian enclaves (or concentrations), which were present in Chicago, Boston and New York after the period of mass migration to the United States between 1880 and 1924, and 'real' ghettos such as the African-American ghettos. In the former, only the Poles in Chicago formed half the population living in such areas, whereas in the latter 'real' ghettos, 80 to 90 per cent of the area populations comprised African Americans in the 1980s and more than three-quarters of the black population lived in such areas (Massey and Denton 1993). These authors have coined the term 'hypersegregation' to describe this situation.

Taking the most strongly concentrated large immigrant population in Sydney, the Vietnam-born, some observations can be made by using data from the 1991 census for the smallest spatial units for which data are available, census collection districts. The average total population size of collection districts is about 750 people and there are about 5,000 of the units in the greater metropolitan area of Sydney. In 1991, there was only one collection district in metropolitan Sydney in which 50 per cent of the population was born in Vietnam and nine in which over 40 per cent were born in Vietnam. While detailed information on the second generation (those born in Australia of Vietnam-born parents) is unavailable at this geographic level, indirect estimates of second generation size can be made by applying the ratio of the second generation to the first generation Vietnam-born populations which were available at the State level. Assuming these proportions apply, the Vietnam origin population almost certainly exceeded 60 per cent of the total population in one collection district in Cabramatta (Fairfield SLA) in Western Sydney, and over 50 per cent of the population in seven collection districts, also in the same area. It is estimated that only 7.6 per cent of the Vietnam origin population in Sydney resided in collection districts in which over half the total population was of Vietnam origin. Furthermore the Vietnam-born population in these areas comprises two ethnic groups: the ethnic Chinese from Vietnam and the ethnic Vietnamese. The Vietnam-origin population itself is heterogeneous. It therefore cannot be suggested that the Vietnam-born population in Sydney is ghettoised. This point is emphasised again by the following comparative observations with reference to the large and more concentrated immigrant groups in Sydney. Only 11 per cent of the Vietnam-born resided in census collection districts in 1991 where they comprised over 20 per cent of the total population, and only six per cent of the Lebanon-born, the next most concentrated of the larger immigrant groups. Indeed, 54 per cent of the Vietnam-born resided in collection districts where they comprised less than 5 per cent of the total population, compared to 61 per cent of the Lebanese-born, 69 per cent of the Greece-born population, 86 per cent of the China-born population and 94 per cent of the Hong Kong-born population. Hence a continuum of relative concentration (or dispersion) is evident with the major European, Middle Eastern and Asia-born groups, and not a categorical jump in level of concentration or segregation. This is despite the fact that the Asia-origin groups are more recent arrivals and thus might be expected to be more residentially concentrated at least on an interim basis, whereas the Europe-origin groups have mostly been resident in Australia for several decades.

Considering settlement numbers at the SLA level, the numbers of Vietnam-born or Lebanon-born in particular areas is not markedly more than with the Greek and Italian populations soon after their arrival in the large-scale migrations of the 1950s and 1960s. At the 1971 census, for example, there were 13,000 Greek-born persons in Marrickville SLA and a further 2,000 Greeks born in Cyprus. All told there were 30,000 first generation Greeks in the contiguous Sydney, Leichhardt, Marrickville, Botany and Randwick (Kensington) SLAs in the inner city, and there were 5,000 Italian-born in Leichhardt and 14,000 in the adjacent inner city SLAs of Leichhardt, Marrickville (Petersham), Drummoyne, and Ashfield (Five Dock) Local Government Areas. In Fairfield-Liverpool there were 12,000 first generation Italians, most from Calabria in the south of Italy, in 1971, and in Fairfield Local Government Area alone there were 12,000 first and second generation Italians in total at the 1976 census, and almost as many at the 1991 census. At the latter census, there were more than 12,000 first and second generation Greeks in an area of second generation settlements (although interspersed with other ethnic communities) in Canterbury SLA in Sydney's inner south. In Melbourne in 1971, soon after the major post-war southern European migration, there were 10,000 Italian-born in Brunswick SLA in the inner northern areas, and over 25,000 Greek-born persons in the adjacent inner southern suburbs of Richmond, Collingwood, Prahran and South Melbourne. There were 5,000 persons born in Yugoslavia in Footscray SLA, and so on.

In 1991, there were 19,000 persons born in Vietnam born in Fairfield SLA in Sydney, the largest single SLA of Vietnam-born in Australia and the largest overseas birthplace grouping in any one SLA in Australia at that date. While the sizeable southern European numbers in particular areas in the 1950s were not seen as ghettos, except in some of the tabloid press as we have seen above, the Indochinese concentrations have been labelled as ghettos by some social scientists. It is interesting, therefore, that the three contiguous areas having both the highest aggregate numbers of persons, and proportion of the total population, born in any overseas country (60 to 70 per cent in a number of census collection districts at the 1976 census) were Elizabeth, Salisbury and Munno Para in Adelaide. The immigrant population in this case comprised persons born in the United Kingdom.

Taking the above figures and discussion together, several conclusions emerge. First, the proportions that individual birthplace groups with their

Australian-born children form of the population of small areas like collection districts is nowhere near as high as that formed regularly by the African-American population in the United States, or the Hispanic Americans in California, south-western United States cities, or in New York. Secondly, all levels of concentration in Australian cities are significantly below that of the Bangladeshi population in Spitalfields in Tower Hamlets, London, reported by Peach (1996, p. 221). Thirdly, the number of SLAs in Australian cities with high concentrations is small, and the number of collection districts with very high concentrations is also limited. Fourthly, the proportions of given birthplace groups living at such high densities are mostly low.

Residential concentration and disadvantage?
– a Sydney case study

English language facility is a key to socioeconomic adjustment in the wider society. Persons with an inadequate command of the host society language may experience difficulty in obtaining work commensurate with their qualifications or sometimes in obtaining any job. Lack of English language proficiency cuts access to information about work and housing opportunities in the wider society. Analysis of data for New South Wales and Australia from the 1991 census clearly shows, more especially with males, that recent arrivals in Australia have a higher proportion with limited English proficiency than long term residents. In Australia in 1991, taking all persons of non English-speaking background in aggregate, the percentage of male residents resident here for 0-4 years and not speaking English well was 16.6 per cent; among the 5-9 years groups it was 10.3 per cent; 10-14 year residents, 8.0 per cent; 15-19 years residents, 7.0 per cent and 20+ year residents, 6.9 per cent. With increasing duration of residence English competency increases. The gradation by duration of residence exists with females but is less marked and a higher proportion of women have limited proficiency than with men. However with all major immigrant groups of non English-speaking background a majority spoke English well in 1991, the proportion being highest with the long-resident German and Dutch settlers and lowest with the Vietnam-born who were more recent arrivals.

At the 1991 census, a significant minority of persons in Australia born in Greece, Italy, Yugoslavia, Lebanon and Turkey could not speak English well, despite their relatively long residence in Australia, with the exception of the Lebanon-born (Australian Bureau of Statistics Census 1991, Table CSC 60109). Meanwhile, substantial minorities (over 40 per cent) of the Vietnam, Laos and Cambodia-born had low English proficiency, reflecting in part the recent arrivals among these communities. These factors should be borne in mind in interpreting Table 3.2 which shows indexes of dissimilarity between persons within major birthplace groups in Sydney who spoke English well and the Australian-born, and those who did not speak English well and the Australian-born. Generally members of major birthplace groups who had limited English proficiency were more residentially concentrated than those members who spoke English well, more especially with those born in China, Greece, Lebanon, Malta or Vietnam. Thus whereas 13 per cent of the metropolitan China-born population resided in Fairfield SLA in 1991, 19 per cent of those not speaking English well resided there. In Marrickville SLA, 17.0 per cent of the Greeks in Sydney with limited English resided compared to 9.8 per cent of the metropolitan Greek population.

Furthermore, English language proficiency differed by gender within ethnic concentration areas and between ethnic concentration areas and other areas of Sydney. Thus with the Vietnam-born in Fairfield SLA in 1991, 45 per cent of males and 56 per cent of females could not speak English well compared to 36 and 44 per cent of Vietnam-born men and women residing outside areas of concentration in Sydney. Among the China-born, 62.6 per cent of males in Fairfield SLA spoke limited English compared to 35.9 per cent outside SLAs of concentration. With Vietnamese women the comparable figures were 70 and 41.7 per cent. Among Lebanon-born women in their primary concentration SLA, Canterbury, 38.6 per cent spoke limited English compared to 29.8 per cent outside SLAs of concentration, while with population born in Greece, 42 per cent of men in their core concentration, Marrickville, spoke limited English compared to 25 per cent outside areas of concentration. For Greek-born women, the equivalent figures were 57 per cent and 29.6 per cent. These strong contrasts between concentration areas cannot wholly be accounted for by differences in recency of arrival in Australia. While there was a trend for recent arrivals to be more resident in ethnic concentrations here they could find social supports to help them adjust to their new milieu, the contrasts in the residential location of recent and long term settlers were not nearly as marked as the English proficiency differences. Many long-resident settlers from southern Europe had stayed in old residential concentrations or relocated to new concentrations. A higher proportion of those less proficient in English may have chosen to do this. And while lesser incomes may have constrained the residential dispersion of some of these longer resident settlers, home ownership was achieved in many residential concentrations. Figures 3.2 to 3.4 show the distributions and concentrations of Vietnamese, Spanish and Khmer speakers in Sydney in 1991 (Table 3.1 shows the boundaries of Sydney's SLAs on which Figures 3.2 to 3.4 are based).

Table 3.2   Indexes of dissimilarity between members of selected birthplace groups speaking English well, not well and the Australian-born in Sydney

Indexes

Birthplace group	Persons not speaking English well	Persons speaking English well
China	47.1	40.2
Greece	55.2	46.1
Hong Kong	42.9	37.4
Italy	38.2	33.6
Lebanon	56.7	48.4
Malta	44.9	
Philippines	38.8	33.2
Poland	35.1	28.7
Former USSR	38.7	33.1
Vietnam	73.4	64.6
Turkey	55.6	42.1
Former Yugoslavia	40.4	35.2

Source: Commonwealth of Australia (various years) (1991)
Note: (1) Spatial units = Statistical Local Areas
(2) Not speaking English well = The combined census categories 'not well' and 'not at all'.

Figure 3.1 Boundaries of Sydney's Statistical Local Areas (SLAs)

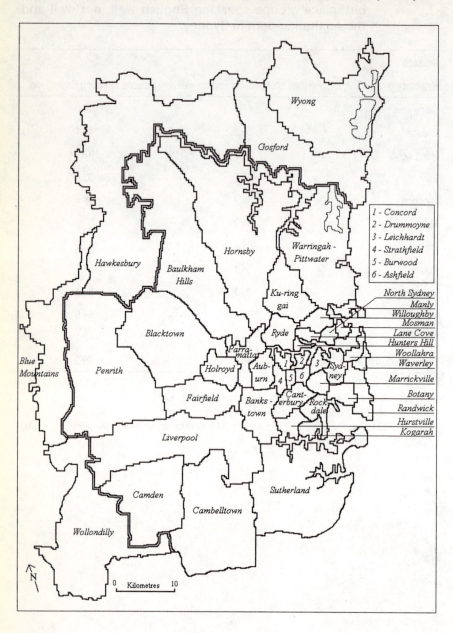

Source: The authors, based on Commonwealth of Australia (various years)

Figure 3.2 Language spoken at home in Sydney 1991: Spanish

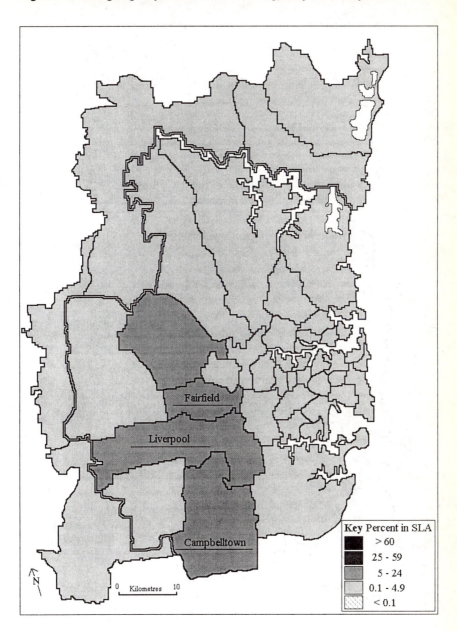

Key Percent in SLA
> 60
25 - 59
5 - 24
0.1 - 4.9
< 0.1

Fairfield

Liverpool

Campbelltown

Source: Australian Bureau of Statistics (1991a)

Figure 3.3 Language spoken at home in Sydney 1991: Vietnamese

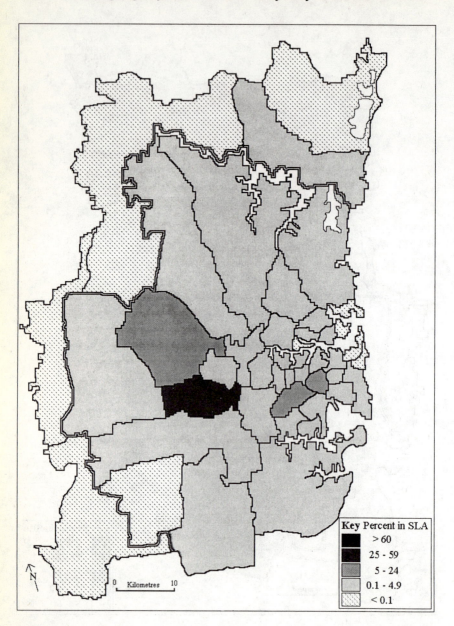

Source: Australian Bureau of Statistics (1991a)

Figure 3.4 Language spoken at home in Sydney 1991: Khmer

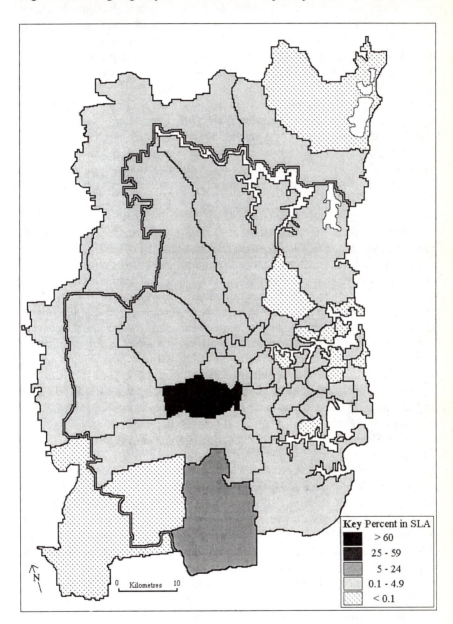

Key Percent in SLA
- > 60
- 25 - 59
- 5 - 24
- 0.1 - 4.9
- < 0.1

Source: Australian Bureau of Statistics (1991a)

It was likely that the English language proficiency issue would influence employment status and thus incomes of persons within and outside ethnic concentration areas and to an extent this has been the case, at least in Sydney, as Table 3.3 indicates. The table displays percentages of male members of birthplace-language groups who were unemployed and seeking work at the 1991 census, and who were resident in an SLA of residential concentration and in other areas of Sydney. Proportions are also quoted for female members of birthplace – language groups. Several features emerge. First, unemployment among groups from China, Vietnam, the Middle East, Macedonia, and South and Central America exceeded that of the Australia-born in each SLA of immigrant concentration. Secondly, at the metropolitan level, unemployment exceeded 40 per cent among the Moslem Arabic-speakers and among the Vietnamese and Khmer groups, and ranged between 25 and 30 per cent among the Chinese-Vietnamese and Arabic-speaking Christians, and was also elevated among the Serbian and Croation speakers. Unemployment, however, was not elevated among the longer resident Greek and Italian speakers, or among the more recently arrived Macedonians. Thirdly, with the Vietnamese, Chinese from Vietnam, and the Khmer and Lao speakers, unemployment in the areas of ethnic concentration was much higher than among compatriots elsewhere in Sydney. The English language difficulties discussed above may have contributed to this. Fourthly, such differentials were stronger among the women in these groups. For example, unemployment among Vietnamese-speaking women exceeded 61 per cent in Fairfield SLA, 64 per cent in Liverpool SLA, and 55 per cent in Marrickville, compared to 44 per cent outside the areas of concentration in Sydney. Unemployment was similarly elevated with the Khmer-speaking women (57.4 per cent in Fairfield where 70 per cent had settled compared to 59.2 per cent in Liverpool, 55 per cent in Marrickville, and 44.2 per cent in other areas of Sydney). It was also elevated among Arabic-speaking Moslem women in concentrations (53.5 per cent in Fairfield and 53.5 per cent in Canterbury) compared to other areas of Sydney (48.7 per cent). In the case of the Moslem Arabic women, work force participation was low (27 per cent): many were at the family-forming stage of the life cycle. However the low participation, as well as reflecting cultural values almost certainly indicated lack of access to culturally appropriate child care, and it may have resulted in persons having given up the search for work. Unemployment among Turkish men exceeded 38 per cent, and in Auburn SLA where 25 per cent of the Turkish-born in Sydney resided, unemployment exceeded 35 and 39 per cent respectively among Turkish men and women. Despite comparatively long residence in Australia since 1966-1976 when most arrived, unemployment remained a serious problem with the Turkish-born. In sum, unemployment levels among Spanish, Vietnamese, Chinese from Vietnam, Lao, Khmer, Moslem Arabic-speakers and Serbian, Croatian and Turkish speakers were

Table 3.3   Percentages of males among major birthplace-language groups unemployed in SLAs of residential concentration, 1991

Statistical Local Area

Language	Birthplace	Fairfield	Bankstown	Liverpool	Canterbury	Marrickville	Other Sydney	Total Sydney
English	Australia	12.0	8.5	12.0	9.0	11.7	7.9	8.7
Spanish	South American	23.5	17.1	26.6	19.9	17.8	13.8	17.9
Italian	Italy	10.9	9.7	13.3	9.5	11.6	8.9	9.5
Arabic (Christian)	Middle East	35.2	30.5	39.8	34.0	30.9	29.5	30.4
Chinese	Vietnam	29.6	24.8	32.6	28.4	22.5	19.8	26.2
Chinese	China	25.0	17.1	11.0	14.3	14.0	8.5	14.6
Vietnamese	Vietnam	46.2	39.3	48.9	35.5	46.4	35.5	41.7
Khmer	all	45.6	39.1	50.1	40.9	47.2	34.4	40.2
Lao	all	31.1	37.9	36.2	34.7	36.2	22.6	28.2
Greek	Greece	18.9	12.1	15.6	13.5	16.7	8.9	11.8
Arabic (Islam)	Middle East	43.9	43.9	40.1	47.1	41.3	44.8	45.1
Macedonian	Yugoslavia*	14.3	9.9	11.1	15.5	17.6	9.7	11.8
Serbian	Yugoslavia	27.0	26.9	18.2	28.1	28.9	19.2	23.3
Croatian	Yugoslavia	15.2	18.0	17.9	18.1	22.8	13.1	15.9

Source: Australian Bureau of Statistics Census (1991b)
Note: *refers to the former Yugoslav Republic

significantly elevated in areas of ethnic concentration, especially in western Sydney. One influence has been structural changes in manufacturing industry in western Sydney in the 1980s (Fagan and Webber 1994) following earlier structural change in inner Sydney industries in the 1970s (Murphy and Watson 1990). These trends are revisited in detail in Chapter 7.

It follows that incomes of certain language-birthplace groups were lower in several SLAs of ethnic concentration than with members of the same groups in other areas of Sydney. Whereas 24 per cent of English-speaking families living in Fairfield SLA were earning below $25,000 in 1991, only 17 per cent were in Sydney. For comparison 37 per cent of Vietnamese-speaking families earned below this figure in Fairfield and 43.5 per cent in Liverpool SLA compared to 23 per cent of Vietnamese-speaking families in other areas of Sydney. Almost 70 per cent of the Khmer speakers were resident in Fairfield, and of Cambodian families in this SLA, 50 per cent were earning below $25,000 compared to 34 per cent of Khmer speakers resident outside areas of residential concentration. In the case of Spanish-speaking families from south and central America, 40 per cent in Liverpool SLA and 30 per cent in Fairfield SLA earned below $25,000 compared to 19 per cent among compatriots outside residential concentration areas. Thus while ghetto conditions do not exist in Sydney, some socioeconomic disadvantage does, and its incidence is higher in some areas of residential concentration, although less so in the case of the established southern European communities. It is not suggested that spatial concentration causes disadvantage, but rather that those likely to experience disadvantage may chose to stay in ethnic concentrations. Lack of facility in English and to an extent recency of arrival may contribute to the higher incidence of disadvantage in some concentration areas. On the other hand, by remaining in residential concentrations, or migrating to them, communal support can be maintained and this may mitigate socioeconomic disadvantage.

Newer approaches to the study of ethnic residential concentration

Newer approaches to the study of ethnic residential concentration have substantially different perspectives on their existence and to a certain extent their causation. Anderson (1991) has argued forcefully that ethnic concentrations such as Vancouver's Chinatown can be 'constructions' of the dominant society rather than the ethnic group in question. Ethnic concentrations can result from prejudice or discrimination on the part of the wider society and Anderson (1993) considers that this has been the case with some groups in Sydney. While it is arguable that Sydney's Chinatown is at least

Table 3.4   **Associations between overseas immigration and intra-urban and internal out-migration rates by SLA in metropolitan Sydney, 1976-1981, 1981-1989 and 1986-1991**

	Pearson's Correlation Coefficients	
Period	Overseas immigration and intra-urban out-migration	Overseas in-migration and internal out-migration
1976-1981	.70**	.50**
1981-1986	.59**	−.42*
1986-1991	.74**	−.38*

Sources: Commonwealth of Australia (various years)
Australian Bureau of Statistics (various years: c)
NSW Valuer General (1976-1991)
Travers Morgan Pty Ltd (1991a)

Notes: (1)   ** significance <0.01
(2)   * significance <0.05
(3)   intra-urban out-migration = out-migration rates from Sydney SLAs to other parts of metropolitan Sydney
(4)   internal out-migration = out-migration rates from Sydney SLAs to areas of Australia outside the metropolitan region
(5)   the immigration variable was the 0-4 years overseas-born resident in Australia cohort at the 1981, 1986 and 1991 censuses.

in part a construction similar to that in Vancouver, it is now largely non-residential yet it is utilised by many persons of Chinese background (and also by many others of non-Chinese background). It is also the focus of many Chinese ethnic voluntary organisations and institutions, although by no means all of them. Certainly it has been fostered by wider societal tourism-entrepreneurship and planning policies, and by foreign investment in recent years, much of which is from Singapore and Hong Kong. Municipal authorities and other State Department of Planning authorities have considered the 'fostering' of 'Chinatowns', as at Chatswood on Sydney's north shore, and at Cabramatta and Ashfield in Sydney's west and inner west (Wang 1993; Inglis and Wu 1993). These newer 'Chinatowns' reflect strong investment from Hong Kong and Singapore, as well as local investment initiatives, but they may have important symbolic significance for many of the regional groupings of recent migrants from China, Taiwan, Malaysia, Singapore and Hong Kong who have settled in

Ashfield-Strathfield and in upper north shore SLAs which are mostly middle to higher income areas. The visibility and symbolic importance of 'Chinatowns', Little Greeces and Little Italies are being reflected, more especially in Melbourne, in planning initiatives for the control and development of 'character areas' and cultural heritage policies (Melbourne Strategy Plan 1985, pp. 57-95). Examples include the Lygon Street Action Plan, the preservation of 'Little Greece' on Lonsdale Street, and Chinatown, the last two of which are in the central business district itself. This shows a strong tolerance for precincts which substantially conform to Anderson's (1991) views concerning the social construction of 'ethnic' institutions, places and spaces. However, the localities mentioned in Melbourne's central business district are not residential concentrations in themselves, although the Lygon Street area in Carlton, immediately north of the central business district, was once the primary focus of Italian residential settlement in Melbourne. It should be noted that the emergent 'Chinatown' pattern in Ashfield-Strathfield and Chatswood in Sydney are not the formalised Chinatowns of the Dixon and Little Bourke Street areas respectively in the Sydney and Melbourne central business districts. The Cabramatta 'China-Vietnam' town is semi-formalised in that municipal and State governments have encouraged the grouping and proliferation of businesses and restaurants and have subsidised public monuments.

An alternative perspective in the study of immigrant settlement involves the use of social network approaches. Network analyses usually examine the metropolitan-wide friendship linkages within or between ethnic group members and members of other groups. For example, Grimes (1982, 1987) examined the wider social networks of Irish immigrants living in one part of Sydney and found it necessary to question the assumption that spatial dispersal (of this group) was synonymous with a high level of assimilation. He found that despite widespread dispersal of the Irish in Sydney, there was a specific 'ethnic' pattern of friendship among Irish men, based particularly on the monopoly of certain lines of work, and that there was a more gradual process of adaptation of many Irish immigrants to their new environment. The work linkages were associated with labouring, semi-skilled workers and tradesmen, particularly plant operators, drainers and pipe layers. Seventy-six per cent of the 484 friends of the Irish samples were also Irish, and this in-group interaction pattern was stronger among recent arrivals. Some network members had established business partnerships as small construction contractors, thus assuring continuity to friendships despite long distances between homes. Such contractors frequently employed younger Irish immigrants, which resulted in a predominantly Irish work environment, and the all-male drinking group, often associated with construction circles, was the main means of sustaining a strong network over a long time, indeed since the 1950s. A strong in-group complex pattern of social interaction occurred between the Irish in inner western Sydney with other residentially dispersed Irish friends. Conversely Burnley (1985) found in a large sample survey of Greek, Italian, Lebanese and 'Yugoslav' settlers in areas of strong concentration at the neighbourhood level in Sydney, that there were strong in-group social interaction patterns with relatives and friends within the ethnic concentrations as well as compatriots living elsewhere. Yet with increasing duration of residence in Australia, considerable acculturation to Australian folkways as indicated by diet, use of English, naturalisation and voting was taking place within the concentrations.

Another recent perspective on immigrant settlement suggests that there can be distinct advantages to the ethnic groups in the concentration of their population in cities. For example, Dunn (1993), with reference to the Vietnamese in Cabramatta in western Sydney, has suggested that their population concentrations actually assist interaction with the broader society. This is because of the social support systems within the ethnic community, and also because public welfare and English language training facilities can be set up locally which can serve an appreciable proportion of the ethnic community. People can also gain access to a range of key facilities as well as services serving specific ethnic concentrations – such as grocers, delicatessens, fruiterers, real estate and business agents, accountants, doctors, taxation agents, travel agents – and this eases stresses on people who are unfamiliar with the language and opportunity structure of the new society in which they find themselves, because they can carry out their day-to-day transactions in their own language. Furthermore, a substantial concentration of ethnic services and small businesses can provide significant employment opportunities for ethnic community members. Indeed Fagan (1993) has commented on the entrepreneurial potential that exists in the residential concentrations of populations from the former Indochina that exist in outer western Sydney and which might generate employment and opportunities for at least some of the community members there (see Chapter 7). In 1996 there were over 700 small businesses owned or operated by persons born in the former Indochina in Fairfield SLA. This follows on a tradition established by continental European ethnic groups there and in the inner city (Castles et al. 1992). For instance in 1996 there were over 600 Italian owned and operated small businesses in the Annandale, Leichhardt, Five Dock and Haberfield localities of the inner city and as many Greek businesses in the Newtown, Marrickville and Lakemba localities in the southern inner suburbs. A positive aspect of these businesses has been their varied nature and the fact that the majority did not exclusively serve a specific ethnic clientele. This reflects the population mixture that exists in areas of strong ethnic concentration. A second positive aspect was that many ethnic small businesses employed a bilingual or multilingual staff and this has fostered communication between different ethnic groups and between immigrant groups and the Australian-origin population. It has often been the policy of ethnic small businesses to hire at least some people with a good command of English, since English-speaking persons are often among regular clientele, depending on the business. Not only do many small businesses flourish on the basis of local ethnic identity but many immigrants have been attracted to settle in specific localities, including Fairfield in western Sydney, because of the ethnic diversity and associated ambience of the area.

Another newer approach to the study of immigrant communities has been to examine the responses of the local, or 'host society' population to the ethnic group presence, particularly the establishment of places of religious worship, cultural and social centres and some businesses (Murphy and Watson 1997). There has been considerable media coverage of opposition on the part of some local communities to the establishment of mosques and associated institutions, for example. Municipal records indicate that the reasons for objects may be the zoning laws, incompatible land uses, car-parking problems or aesthetic factors, as when a tower may dominate a residential district. Such objections tend to occur in newer residential districts into which an ethnic community may be relocating or suburbanising. Sometimes there is another agenda behind the objections. It follows that the result of such objections may be to impede residential dispersion of immigrants and to reinforce ethnic concentrations. Many of the objectives, however, are overcome and the conflicts resolved through democratic and community consultative procedures.

A further perspective on ethnic concentration focuses more on the subjective meaning of place to new arrivals from different milieux and physical environments. In this sense, an ethnic concentration area with its visual symbols – ethnic churches, chapel, clubs, advertising and business signs written in the ancestral language, often using the ancestral script, restaurants and cafes – become a familiar, 'feel at home' locale, for its inhabitants and often for members of the same ethnic group who live elsewhere in the urban area but visit the concentration area from time to time. The concentration area becomes a distinctive milieu symbolically and actually for its inhabitants, as they adjust to their new environment. It given them a sense of continuity with their past and eases the pain of coming to terms with an often very different social and urban setting.

Conclusion

It is clear that the share of immigrants in the population of Australia's metropolitan cities is comparatively high on an international scale, given that Australia has the highest proportion of overseas-born in its population of any nation in the world, apart from Israel, and that much of the immigration, especially that of persons of non English-speaking background, is strongly metropolitan-focussed. The three metropolitan cities most impacted by immigration in the last 20 years have been Sydney, Melbourne and Perth, and this is reflected in settlement at the neighbourhood level within the cities. It is interesting here that whereas metropolitan Toronto in Canada, a city of the same population size as Sydney, had 40 per cent of its population born overseas in 1991, Sydney's overseas-born were estimated to comprise almost 35 per cent of the total population in 1996. Neither metropolis has substantial ethnic segregation or large areas of poverty.

Despite the strong immigrant focus within Australia on Sydney and Melbourne, significant residential concentrations and communities exist in other cities, for example, the Vietnam-born in Darra in Brisbane, the Macedonians and Turks in Cringila and adjacent areas in Wollongong, and Serbs and Croats in Port Adelaide. The analysis has shown that no major birthplace group can be shown as being segregated in Australian cities, as indicated by indexes of dissimilarity, although strong residential concentrations exist. Not only is there no situation in which anywhere near all of a given birthplace group resides in any one SLA but there is no contemporary grouping of census collection districts in which more than 30 to 40 per cent of the total population is comprised of the same immigrant group. The group which does show a 30 to 40 per cent concentration is the Vietnamese-born in the Cabramatta area of Fairfield SLA in western Sydney in 1991. Other immigrant groups and Australian-born were also resident there, although some out-migration of Australian-born has been occurring (Birrell 1993). The net internal migration losses experienced by Fairfield SLA between 1986 and 1991, and mentioned by Birrell, are however part of a much wider pattern of internal migration losses which have occurred in metropolitan Sydney in recent years as the result of counter-urbanisation migration (Sant and Simons 1993; Hugo 1994; Burnley 1996a), as well as interstate migration to Queensland. Indeed 32 of the 43 SLAs of metropolitan Sydney experienced net internal migration losses between 1986 and 1991, including Fairfield, Liverpool, and Blacktown in western Sydney. The internal migration losses have been found to be not significantly related to overseas-born immigration by area (Burnley 1996b) although intra-urban migration losses are. However, this reflects the replacement factor discussed in the previous chapter whereby many immigrants settle in established areas which are being vacated selectively by native Australian-born or other immigrants as they move to satisfy housing aspirations appropriate to their stage of the life cycle.

There has been sharp debate over the significance of ethnic concentrations and whether some of them may be ghettos in the process of formation. Jupp, and also Viviani and Coughlan, have argued that ghettos are not forming in Australian cities, using Jupp, McRobbie and York's (1990) influential definition of ghettos as a criterion. In any case, the word ghetto is a Yiddish word and refers to Jewish quarters of eastern European cities which existed before and during the Second World War. One attribute of these ghettos, apart from their being designated by authorities as such, was that they became havens because of discrimination and persecution in the wider world. They became areas of residence of last resort. While Harlem in new York may be regarded as a ghetto in this sense, immigrant concentration areas in Australian cities have not become places of last resort.

This is not to say that socioeconomic disadvantage is not associated with some immigrant concentrations in Australian cities. Such associations do not mean that the ethnic concentrations in themselves cause disadvantage or social separation. Key factors in disadvantage in many areas of western Sydney and in comparable areas of Melbourne and Adelaide have been industrial restructuring and the loss of many unskilled and semi-skilled jobs in those sections of manufacturing industry in which immigrants with lesser education and skills, and a less adequate command of English, have commonly had to find employment. With reference to industry, it is necessary for government to target services to local small- to medium-sized enterprises to boost their competitiveness. Further regional developments are required in the industrial outer areas of the cities to build upon existing industry networks and specialisations, to boost local economic capacity to pursue economic and employment growth, and to overcome initial impediments to the establishment of local enterprises. Such initiatives might best be taken through collaboration between the Federal and State governments.

A connection between strong ethnic residential concentration, high unemployment and therefore disadvantage is the degree of English language proficiency. Higher proportions of persons not speaking English well were evident in the Lebanese, Vietnamese and Turkish core concentrations in Sydney, notably among women, and higher levels of unemployment were experienced in these concentrations as well, more especially with women. Persons with less spoken English or capacity to read it have less chance of obtaining information about opportunities in their wider environment, or of obtaining work. Many immigrants from non English-speaking backgrounds settle in, and may elect to stay in ethnic concentration areas if they have limited English language capacity. They can conduct their basic shopping and essential business in their ancestral language as well as obtaining informal and formal social support in their local neighbourhoods. There may thus be less incentive to learn English. However, there may be constraints on the learning of English. Many immigrants arrive in Australia at the family forming stage of the life cycle and for women in particular, there are often difficulties in finding time and circumstances to attend English classes. For example, there is an acute shortage of culturally appropriate child care provision so that women with young children cannot avail themselves of the opportunities to attend English language classes. Likewise, for many immigrants who come to Australia as refugees and are thus virtually penniless on arrival, the men have to obtain what work they can, sometimes two or three casual part-time jobs at once, and with the travelling involved, often by public transport, there simply is insufficient time left for sustained attendance of English classes. Many of these observations also apply to family reunion migrants, for many of these from the Middle East, South Asia, South-East Asia and South America have been defacto refugees, or have arrived in Australia with limited economic resources.

It follows that there needs to be not only substantially more provision of English language instruction at convenient locations at different times of the day and week to allow effective participation by migrants, abut there needs to be continuing government supports and benefits to allow men and women to attend these classes. Unfortunately, at times of economic difficulty, State and Federal governments tend to cut English classes and the like as a relatively soft option to save money. Furthermore there is evidence that with immigrants having markedly different linguistic backgrounds than English, it takes considerably longer for the average persons to obtain a good working knowledge of English. There is limited availability of graduated language classes for such people.

The recent tightening of English language requirements for certain categories of immigrants by the new Coalition Federal Government may in the long term result in increased numbers and proportions of immigrants from diverse backgrounds having a good working knowledge of English. However these changes are more with the 'concessional' family reunion category and 'skilled' migration categories rather than the preferential migration category. With the concessional category, which involves more distant relatives than the preferential family reunion category, intending immigrants will have to demonstrate some knowledge of English to be allowed to settle. The government rightly has not imposed this requirement on the preferential category, which can involve elderly dependent relatives such as parents in some cases, since such imposition could lack humanity. It may be arguable that fiancees or spouses/partners of migrants should be required to pass English language tests before migration. Nevertheless, it will be necessary to increase and extend access to affordable English language instruction in Australia in the foreseeable future.

Finally, the cutting of unemployment and welfare benefits to recurrently-arrived immigrants, other than refugees, which has been undertaken by the new Federal Government, should be examined. There is considerable hardship for persons who are sponsored by lower income persons, who are often former refugees, in the family reunion category. Many have language problems, have limited assets and experience stresses related to those of migrants who are formally refugees. Limiting benefits will not make their social and economic adjustments easier in Australia's urban society.

chapter four

Urban infrastructure and planning

A spokesman for the NSW Planning Minister, Mr Webster, said the Federal Government was providing inadequate funding for Sydney's infrastructure needs. The Opposition Leader, Mr Carr, said the immigration flow was placing enormous pressure on Sydney's aging infrastructure. (Millett 1994)

Senator Bolkus [the then Australian Immigration Minister] believes that NSW is overstating its case in an attempt to wrest more money out of the Commonwealth. (Millett and Armitage 1994)

[T]he answer to the question of infrastructure costs cannot be found by seeking to limit physical growth [of Sydney]. Part of the answer lies in altering the proportions of those costs borne by the various sectors of government, by the private sector and by the users of services. (Greiner 1990)

When immigrants settle in cities they obviously add to demand for urban infrastructure and services in all their forms. In broad terms the needs of recent immigrants are, however, no different to those of the 'host' population which of course includes earlier immigrants. There are indeed categories of 'ethno-specific' demand beyond the norm – interpreter services and the teaching of English as a second language, for example – but these represent only a very small part of total needs. Immigration has nevertheless been adversely linked in Australia with public concerns about the provision of urban infrastructure and the services which flow from it. In essence this linkage stems from the fact that State and Local governments, which in Australia have traditionally constructed and operated most urban infrastructure and services, have faced increased difficulties in financing them over the past 20 years or so. Certain types of urban infrastructure are, as a result, considered to be inadequately supplied and maintained. In order to cope with demands, governments are turning to electorally unpopular methods involving cost-recovery pricing and the privatisation of government agencies. The assumption is made by some that demand pressures resulting from immigration reinforce these trends. Accordingly, the political representatives of those States and Local Government Areas where recent immigrants concentrate tend to argue that they have inadequate resources to cope with demand for infrastructure and services.

In order to locate the relationship between immigration, urban infrastructure and urban services in an appropriate context, several matters need to be addressed. Accordingly, this chapter, after first defining what is meant by urban infrastructure, outlines the conditions which have generated public debate about the provision of infrastructure and the services derived from it in Australia, the responsibilities and financial capacities of different levels of government in Australia with respect to urban infrastructure and services, and the implications of immigration for this. The chapter also reviews attention given to infrastructure matters in recent metropolitan planning and service delivery strategies. In broad terms the chapter aims to assess the implications of immigrant settlement patterns for the manageability of demands made on suppliers of urban infrastructure and the services which derive from it.

Urban infrastructure and services

Urban infrastructure is simply the hardware or, in economic jargon, the fixed capital that supports the production and consumption of goods and services in cities; in many cases the same item of infrastructure may be used for both activities. Consumption infrastructure – supporting health, recreational and educational services, for example – is particularly relevant when the demands of recent immigrants are being considered. Since, however, immigrants take jobs and run businesses, they also create, directly and indirectly, demand for productive infrastructure.

> A distinction is generally made between utilities and social infrastructure. Examples of the former include roads, railways, power-generation facilities, telecommunication lines, waste treatment facilities and sewerage; and the latter include facilities supporting the provision of health, education, law and order and other community services. (Kirwan 1991)

In practical terms, however, there is no difference between social and physical infrastructure and services. For suppliers, the problems are to identify levels of future demand, including its likely location, and to determine how it should be financed.

The most spatially extensive, and therefore visually most obvious, category of infrastructure in cities is housing. However, reflecting practice in urban environmental management itself, we have found it more convenient to treat housing separately – in Chapter 5. Housing is also distinctive compared with other forms of urban infrastructure because, in Australia, about 95 per cent of it is provided by the private sector (Paris 1993).

Why infrastructure provision and financing are on the public agenda

Governments world-wide have historically constructed and debt-financed urban infrastructure and this has certainly been the case in Australia. For three reasons, however, their capacity to continue operating in this way has diminished over the past quarter century. Kirwan (1990) summarises the reasons for this. First, long term interest rates on borrowings are now higher as a result of the global explosion of demand for capital. Secondly, there are burgeoning, and largely unplanned for, replacement and refurbishment needs for urban infrastructure that was built in the early decades of the present century and even in the 19th century. Notable here are water and sewerage mains and inner city roads that were not designed to accommodate anything like their present volumes of traffic. Thirdly, accelerating concern about environmental deterioration can in part be dealt with by investment in various types of urban infrastructure such as sewerage treatment works and public transport. In Australia, and to varying degrees in the rest of the western industrialised world, slowed rates of economic growth since the early 1970s have slowed growth in tax revenues and thus further exacerbated the difficulties faced by governments charged with infrastructure provision.

In addition to the explicitly urban dimension which is most directly relevant to the concerns of this book, the national infrastructure question has been addressed in various ways in recent years in Australia. At the national level the following matters have been considered (Economic Planning and Advisory Council 1988):

- Whether the national stock of productive infrastructure (such as ports, airports and freeways) – whether in cities or otherwise – is adequate to support economic growth.

- The inadequacy of domestic savings to support capital demand from public and private sectors and the resulting extent to which borrowing to meet infrastructure needs adds to Australia's foreign debt.

The extent to which demand for consumption-related infrastructure – especially housing – 'crowds out' (makes more expensive) the provision of productive infrastructure. The issue here is that capital tied up in producing housing, including support infrastructure, may increase the expense of borrowing to build infrastructure for direct business applications. There is an obvious connection here with immigration.

The provision and financing of urban infrastructure and services

Within this national macro-economic context central questions related to urban infrastructure and the services derived from it are: first, can demands be met; and secondly, by whom should infrastructure be provided and how should its provision and maintenance be financed?

Can demands for urban infrastructure and services be met?

Historically, governments in Australia have financed urban infrastructure and services only partly from charges levied on its users. Much of the resource costs of provision have been covered from general taxation revenue. The pressures noted above have led governments to privatise provision or – and this amounts to the same thing as far as users are concerned – to charge prices which bear a closer relationship to the costs of constructing and maintaining infrastructure; this the so-called 'user pays' principle. Needless to say, electorates have not been overly impressed with these trends, and the matter is taken up below. Depending, however, on the state of the Australian economy, demands for infrastructure and urban services can clearly be met if consumers are willing to cover capital investment and operating costs. In other words, there is no reason why immigration at any level can be construed as creating unmanageable demand for urban services. This is clearly so when immigration creates benefits exceeding costs at the national level, as is generally recognised to be the case (Nieuwenhuysen 1990). Rather, it is a presumed regional variation in the costs and benefits accruing from immigration – a little-researched topic (see Lewis 1992) – that creates the basis for political claims and counter claims.

By whom are urban infrastructure and services financed?

Putting aside for the moment questions of cost recovery pricing and privatisation, a key issue in the Australian context concerns the relationship between the three levels of government: Commonwealth, State and Local. Apart from the private sector, urban infrastructure is overwhelmingly constructed, maintained and financed by State and Local governments with varying levels of direct cost recovery from its users. Other than some airports, defence facilities, some major highways, public housing and universities, the Commonwealth government has no direct role as a supplier or financer of urban infrastructure.

> In 1991, the States were responsible for 62 per cent of national capital spending on infrastructure [urban and otherwise], compared to the Commonwealth with 24 per cent of spending responsibilities and Local Government with 14 per cent. (Commonwealth Industry Commission 1993, p. 12)

Because the Commonwealth government controls immigration, while State and Local governments provide most urban infrastructure and services, there is however constant debate – exemplified in the quotations which opened this chapter – as to whether the Commonwealth distributes sufficient funds to cover costs accrued by the 'lower' levels of government.

Commonwealth–State financial relations

The Commonwealth government – due to its monopoly over personal and company income taxes – raises more revenue than it requires to fund its own operations. State governments, in contrast, raise only about half of what they need from their own revenue sources. The Commonwealth accordingly returns a large quantity of revenue to the States, using as a guideline formulae devised by the Commonwealth Grants Commission (CGC). Revenue is returned in the forms of General Revenue and Specific Purpose Payments. One issue for the States is the total quantum of revenue which is provided, the other is the method of distribution used by the Commonwealth. The total quantum returned to the States has been dropping in real terms as the Commonwealth government has sought to balance its own books. Figure 4.1 shows the situation for New South Wales in the second half of the 1990s, a period during which, as noted above, there was a major boom in immigration which especially 'favoured' Sydney.

In 1994-1995, $17.7 billion worth of General Revenue Grants were returned to the States. The funds are distributed so as to enable an equal quality of services to be provided by the States, irrespective of their own financial capacity and the scale of task involved. This is the so-called principle of 'fiscal equalisation'. As an example, in lightly populated States with large land areas, such as Queensland and Western Australia, the costs of constructing and maintaining non-urban roads to a uniform standard are much greater than in New South Wales and Victoria yet the State tax bases are smaller. Were the States not compensated by the Commonwealth their populations would experience poorer roads. Alternatively, if roads were maintained to the same standard as elsewhere then other services would have to suffer. Such considerations result in wide disparities in per capita grants from the Commonwealth to the States (Table 4.1). It is notable that both New South Wales and Victoria, the States which have traditionally taken the largest share of immigrants, have the lowest per capita revenue from the Commonwealth.

Figure 4.1 Total payments and allocations to New South Wales from the Commonwealth government as a percentage of gross State product, 1985-1992

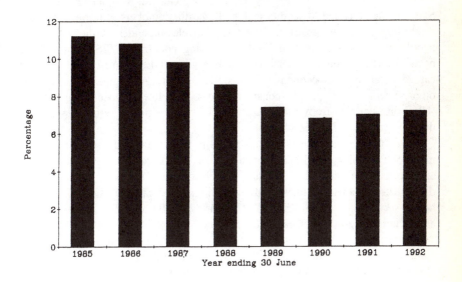

Source: Murphy P.A. (1993)

Table 4.1   Financial assistance grants from Commonwealth to States, A$ per capita, 1989-1990 and 1991-1992

State	1989-1990	1991-1992
New South Wales	628	611
Victoria	619	601
Queensland	844	880
Western Australia	920	949
South Australia	971	1020
Tasmania	1101	1196
Northern Territory	4134	4492

Source: NSW Government (1989 and 1992)

Figures such as these make it easy to understand why there is an important politics of Commonwealth–State financial relationships in Australia and why the implications of immigration are readily factored into that discourse.

A key concept used by the CGC in allocating General Revenue Grants to the States is the so-called 'disability factor'. Regarding numbers of immigrants as a disability, for the purposes of the CGC, the relevant index is the number of people born overseas in non English-speaking countries (NESBs) who have been resident in Australia for less than five years. NESBs are considered in a category called 'socioeconomic factors', along with Aboriginals and various other categories of people considered to be of low socioeconomic status. 'Disabilities arising from differences in social composition were first assessed in the 1981 review' (CGC 1994, p. 189)

The CGC devotes substantial resources to the problem of determining how much of a disability NESBs are for the States, but the commission still has only an approximate idea of the scale of their effects. Details of research into disabilities associated with schools education, technical education, police and health services are contained in CGC reports of 1994 and 1995. These reports also detail further research called for by the CGC.

Special Purpose Payments (SPPs) are negotiated between the Commonwealth and the States from time to time and now comprise half of all Commonwealth payments to the States. Some services for immigrants are provided for by SPPs (e.g. direct Commonwealth funding of English as a Second Language programs in State schools). In other cases NESBs are not the recipients of specialist programs but rather are considered to impose additional costs in the provision of 'mainstream' services. The proportion of a State's population that is NESB is then used as an input in the calculation of disability factors. These factors can relate to either a higher level of demand for a service by NESBs, or a higher unit cost of providing the service to NESBs (CGC 1993, p. 26)

There are, of course, some differences of opinion between the States as to how the immigrant presence should be accounted for in allocation of Commonwealth grants. In general terms, New South Wales and Victoria, the major immigrant States, believe the factor should be given more emphasis while Queensland and South Australia argue for a reduction in weights for NESB (CGC 1994, p. 190)

In the current period of fiscal constraint in Australia, the politics of State–Federal financial relations mean that States are especially pressured to use whatever arguments are at hand – including the impacts of immigration – to lever more money from the Commonwealth. New South Wales and Victoria, in particular, note differential per capita payments to the States (Table 4.1) and argue that, while these may have been justified in earlier decades, they are no longer reasonable.

Russell Matthews' (1992) pioneering study of the impact of immigration on State budgets analysed the relationship in long and shorter term time-frames. He estimated State government expenditure and revenue flows attributable to the Australian-born and the overseas-born components of the population. He split the overseas-born into English-speaking and non English-speaking components. Regarding long-term budgetary effects, Matthews concluded that 'most immigrants are not imposing an undue financial burden on the States at existing levels of service' (Matthews 1992, pp. xix-xx). In 1989-1990 the implied budget deficit for the overseas-born as a whole was estimated to be only about half that of the Australian-born, largely due to higher revenue-raising through taxes and charges. There was a small per capita surplus for the English-speaking group of overseas-born. Even the NESB group's deficit was less than that of the Australian-born. There were expenditure differentials between groups. In the case of health services, the overseas-born incurred higher per capita expenditures in respect of public hospitals but lower expenditure was incurred on other services. In education, the overseas-born incurred much lower expenditure than the Australian-born, except in technical education.

In the shorter term Matthews judges the picture as not so sanguine. He estimated:

> the present financial capacity of State governments is not adequate to provide education, housing and other services on the scale needed by many immigrants if they are to be fully integrated into Australian society.

To the extent that those needs derive directly from the immigration program there is clearly an argument for more Commonwealth funding. The problem, though, appears to be more the overall level of funding than the method of distribution to the States.

Matthews concludes his study as follows (1992, p. xxiv):

> Related to the need for better financial information [the quality of which Matthews criticises strongly] is a need for better coordination of Commonwealth and State Policies. This arises because the Commonwealth determines immigration policy but the States have the responsibility for providing most of the services which immigrants need; and because the Commonwealth receives most of the revenues which immigrants contribute through their taxes but the States incur most of the expenditures. *The widely held belief that Commonwealth grants are provided on a basis that enables States to meet immigrant needs is false.* [Emphasis added. It should be noted that this conclusion does not contradict the points made above about the methods of the CGC. Matthews is concerned with the overall volume of funds rather than the methods by which they are distributed between the States.]
>
> The policies of fiscal restraint which have been adopted by the Commonwealth in recent years are incompatible with a continuing high level of immigration . . .

Of particular concern is the continued admission of large numbers of poorly educated immigrants and the failure to provide resources on the scale necessary if all immigrants are to become literate in English, have access to employment, participate fully in Australian society and achieve standards of living comparable to those of the existing population.

Commonwealth–Local financial relations

Local government in Australia provides a wide range of urban infrastructure and services, including local roads and drainage systems, libraries, child care facilities and the like. Compared with other countries though, notably the United States, Local government's role is residual and, as noted above, accounts for only 14 per cent of national spending on infrastructure. Major urban infrastructure and public services are supplied by the States. This is important because it means that the size of local tax bases is a much less important determinant of service availability and quality – and therefore people's welfare – than it is in some other parts of the world (Murphy and Watson 1994). The financial capacity of Local government has nevertheless been limited for several years with rate (property tax) increases – the main source of revenue – being capped below inflation by fiat from State governments. Since immigrants disproportionately favour some localities over others as places to live, any extra demand for services in those places may, in the present fiscal environment, create difficulties (Cutts 1992).

A related issue which needs to be addressed here concerns the role of Local government as a provider of human services. Traditionally Local government has been regarded as supplying roads, local drainage and waste disposal services. Over recent years many councils have, however, extended their roles to embrace non-traditional human services. While the advocates of this trend will point to its many benefits it has to be recognised that if councils were to stick to their traditional engineering and town planning functions then the financial pressures on them would be less than they are. It may be unkind to suggest this, but to some extent the current financial pressures may regarded as being of councils' own making.

The Commonwealth contributes directly to Local government to varying degrees across States under the Commonwealth *Local Government (Financial Assistance) Act* 1995 and its predecessors. In 1995-1996, A\$1.16 billion was distributed under this arrangement although, proportional to national GDP, this amount has been declining since the early 1980s (NSW Local Government Grants Commission 1995). Funds are distributed through State governments to councils according to formulae devised by State Local Government Grants Commissions. Formulae include a weighting for NESB populations but this is very small. It is recognised that immigrants do make an impact on Local government services but it is considered to be very small relative to overall budgets. Demands include the provision of multilingual information, ethnic affairs officers (partly funded by councils), specialised librarians and community workers. But on the whole 'ethno-specific' services are regarded as constituting only a small proportion of council budgets in areas of high immigrant numbers.

Problems in financing service provision relate much more to the low socioeconomic status of populations in some Local Government Areas rather than to the particular requirements of immigrants who may live there. Financial Assistance Grants as a proportion of Local government revenue accordingly range from less than 3 per cent to over 20 per cent among, for example, Sydney councils. It is notable, however, that high percentages are found in councils with substantial immigrant populations, such as Marrickville, Fairfield and Canterbury. These also happen to be areas of lower than average socioeconomic status and so are more financially constrained. This is particularly so in Fairfield which is a fast-growing outer-suburban area and thus requires large investment in new urban infrastructure. Not only do the populations in areas like Fairfield have a relatively low capacity to pay for services, but the demand for services is growing rapidly. The situation is mirrored in parts of other Australian cities. Not only do immigrants in some localities create a substantial part of the demand for locally supplied infrastructure, they also suffer from inadequacies in supply.

Cost recovery pricing and privatisation of urban infrastructure

Whatever the quantum of funds distributed from one level of government to another, and whatever the methods used to determine the distribution of those funds, there is no question that governments are stepping away from supplying urban infrastructure and services, or else are instituting cost-recovery pricing arrangements. Both methods are politically fraught since they imply higher prices to consumers and because a significant proportion of the Australian electorate supports public ownership of key capital assets. Due to immigration's major role in driving population growth in the larger Australian cities, and in particular localities within those cities, it has readily become a scapegoat for these unpopular trends. The notion seems to be that if immigration were to be curtailed then privatisation and price increases would not need to occur or, at least, their implementation might be delayed. The latter is the only logically defensible position and in any case the long term situation – according to Matthews – appears clearly to be that immigrants impose no more demand on service providers than do the rest of the population. Further consideration of these matters is deferred to Chapter 6 where the relationship between urban environmental quality and immigration is considered. In that chapter the matter of externality pricing, which is a facet of cost-recovery pricing, is discussed. Issues of social equity and urban management related to cost-recovery pricing are also considered there.

Urban growth management, infrastructure provision and immigration

This chapter has so far focussed on the financing of urban infrastructure and services and related intergovernmental arrangements. The management of growth and change in Australian cities – the responsibility for which rests entirely with State and Local governments – intersects with the provision and financing of urban infrastructure and services in important ways. A sketch of these relationships provides further context for a balanced interpretation of the effects of immigration on Australian cities.

Adequacy of demand information

The timely provision of urban infrastructure and services requires high-quality population forecasts. Since immigration is controlled by the Commonwealth government, the States that receive most immigrants have perennially complained about the need for better information on proposed future immigration levels. But no matter how good the communications are on this matter, the fluctuating nature of the immigration intake into Australia means that this element of population growth will remain difficult to forecast. While the intake is set by the Commonwealth government, numbers of potential immigrants are related to economic conditions in Australia and to economic and political conditions in countries of origin. The difficulties of predicting these fluctuations in demand are especially significant for infrastructure planning, which in some cases requires long lead times. These matters were discussed in some detail in Chapter 2.

Within cities, as was noted in Chapter 3, immigrants cluster to varying degrees. While the overseas born have essentially the same needs for urban services there are, at the margin, special needs which have to be dealt with. This applies primarily to human services such as health, education, housing and policing. As the Commonwealth Department of Human Services and Health (1994, p. 23) has stated, 'provision of culturally appropriate services presents a major challenge for service providers'. Each of the agencies involved in meeting such needs thus predicates its service provision on detailed knowledge of birthplace groups in localities. There are many examples of planning studies undertaken by human services agencies and there now seems to be a good understanding of 'ethno-specific' needs – although not always the funds to meet those needs. The manner in which the funding that flows from Commonwealth to State and Local governments is calibrated by the incidence of overseas persons in populations has been described above. Reference has also been made to the adequacy or otherwise of those flows of this funding.

Urban growth management, urban infrastructure and urban services

Recent publications of Australian and State governments list key planning issues directly or indirectly related to the provision of urban infrastructure and services. In a monograph written for the National Housing Strategy, Kirwan (1991, p. ix) highlighted some of the most frequently voiced concerns:

- Areas of new urban development, particularly at the periphery of Sydney and Melbourne, have been allowed to develop without appropriate infrastructure and the provision is often too late;

- The maintenance and replacement of existing infrastructure has been neglected to the point where the cost of overcoming deficiencies will become a major drain on public funds within the foreseeable future;

- The lack of adequate infrastructure in many recently developed areas – a prime source of inequity – can be traced to the lack of an efficient pricing and financing system. Infrastructure is lacking exactly because on present pricing policies there is inadequate finance to undertake the investment necessary to ensure that all new areas of development – and indeed many existing ones – are properly provided with infrastructure.

- The lower cost of housing that has resulted has been achieved only at the cost of inadequate provision of infrastructure where it is particularly needed – the areas where young lower-income and less self sufficient households find their housing.

- The lower price of serviced land has also been a primary cost of urban sprawl.

The linkage drawn by some (Birrell and Tonkin 1992) between these problems and immigration runs as follows: where immigration is a major factor in metropolitan population growth it is directly and indirectly fuelling household formation and thus demand for infrastructure and services at the edge of cities. This process was discussed in Chapter 2. It does not follow, however, that immigration *causes* the problems faced by suppliers of infrastructure. That would only be the case if adequate financing capacity did not exist in metropolitan – that is, in practice, State – tax bases. If, at the national level, the long-run benefits of immigration exceed its costs, as is generally regarded to be the case, and if financial flows from Commonwealth to

State and Local governments properly reflect demand pressures arising from immigration, there should not be a problem. Of course, in the shorter run, if demand unexpectedly increases then there may be pressures of an organisational and financial nature. The former is unavoidable but, since immigration is highest when the Australian economy is growing most strongly, there ought to be the capacity to cope financially.

In its report on the impacts of taxation and financial policy on urban settlement, the Commonwealth Industry Commission (1993, p. 11) concluded, on the question of whether urban sprawl on the edges of Australian cities is subsidised:

> From the information available to it, the Commission considers that urban fringe development is not heavily subsidised overall, particularly in relation to other urban areas.

To the extent that there is subsidy, its elimination:

> would certainly ... increase the value of already serviced properties. But because there would be an 'excess supply' of serviced properties at the new cost level, actual prices would increase only slowly as the overall level of demand for housing grew.

In other words, the move to cost-recovery pricing of urban infrastructure is unlikely to be socially disruptive to a major degree. Furthermore, demand arising from immigration is not being significantly subsidised by general tax payers.

An important Commonwealth government program in the 1990s has been the Australian Urban and Regional Policy Review. In a report on matters pertaining to urban infrastructure, one of the contributors (Neutze 1994, p. 37) opined:

> My own view of an efficient big metropolitan area is one in which employment is located in nodes throughout the urban area so that it is relatively close to where most people live. I think that's the way most Australian cities and cities throughout the world are developing. It is the way I think efficient investment in urban infrastructure will move cities, and I think *it is a way in which efficient pricing of infrastructure services will also tend to push them* [emphasis added].

The point of observations such as this is that to the extent that immigration-driven demand for urban infrastructure is coped with by accelerating the shift to cost-recovery pricing, more efficient cities will result. This point is taken up again in relation to urban environmental management in Chapter 6.

Turning now to the State level, the late 1980s and early 1990s saw reviews of the strategic planning frameworks for the major Australian cities which receive the highest shares of immigrants. As was argued in Chapter 1, the situation in the Sydney region, Australia's largest city and the disproportionate attractor of recent immigrants, is of particular relevance. The following observations were made about infrastructure and services (NSW Department of Planning 1993, pp. 49-50):

> [A key aim of the new strategy is to] promote more efficient use of infrastructure by housing a high proportion of new residents within existing areas. . .
>
> [P]ricing and financing of infrastructure will be crucial elements . . . particularly reducing the rate of fringe growth. Impacts on urban form and environmental quality and the need for greater efficiency will be important considerations in the reviews of infrastructure pricing currently being undertaken by the Government Pricing Tribunal. . .
>
> [C]urrent management and coordination mechanisms have often failed to ensure that human services are readily accessible to residents of new urban areas.

What is notable about this text is that inadequate financial capacity is not flagged by the State agency responsible for planning the metropolitan region. Nor is there any explicit connection made with immigration-fuelled population growth. Similarly, in the metropolitan planning strategy itself, *Cities for the 21st Century: Integrated Urban Management for Sydney, Newcastle, the Central Coast and Wollongong* (NSW Government 1995) no mention is made of infrastructure-financing problems nor any impacts of immigration thereon. Metropolitan planning documents for Melbourne (Ministry for Planning and Environment 1987), Perth (State Planning Commission of Western Australia 1987) and Brisbane (Queensland Department of Housing, Local Government and Planning 1994) produced in the late 1980s and early 1990s, just before and after the most recent immigration boom, also failed to highlight adverse implications of immigration although they did recognise its importance in population growth and in household formation. Speeches made by the premiers of those States at the Bureau of Immigration Research's National Outlook Conference on Immigration in 1990 similarly failed to use what would have been a major opportunity to flag any adverse effects of immigration on State finances and urban management generally.

Conclusion

As was demonstrated in Chapters 2 and 3, immigration contributes substantially to population growth and household formation across and within major Australian cities and thus to demand for urban infrastructure and services. Australia's three-tiered system of government, with its differential financial capacities and responsibilities for urban infrastructure provision, and control over the immigration program, ensure a constant process of bargaining between, especially, the States and the Commonwealth. While there is never enough money to go around – due to rising expectations on the part of the Australian population – and while the mechanisms for financial allocation are based on information of variable quality, the process as a whole is fair and reasonable. The debate about immigration's effects is underpinned by the strained financial capacities of all three levels of government in Australia. In essence this situation results from weak economic growth over the period of national economic restructuring which has been under way since the early 1970s.

The most authoritative review of the impacts of immigration on State budgets (Matthews 1992) concluded that immigration does not place undue burdens on the States in the longer run although this assumes levels of service which may not be considered adequate. There are, however, significant short-term budgetary impacts which are not compensated for by Commonwealth allocations. Because of Sydney's pre-eminent role as the preferred site for recent immigrants, much of the public debate about immigration's supposed effects has come from that city, As the quotation from (former) New South Wales Premier Greiner, at the commencement of this chapter shows, however, the problems which some argue derive from immigration are more apparent than real.

In order to understand how immigration affects Australian cities, some knowledge is required of the issues city planners are grappling with. This chapter of the book has raised the extent to which services to the growth areas in the outer city are under-provided and has linked this, on the one hand, to pricing regimes that do not cover the resource costs of provision and, on the other hand, to the particular spatial structure of Australian cities. Immigration may indeed be linked to these matters. Most significantly, it may be argued that immigration-fuelled population growth has exacerbated the difficulties arising from other sources for governments wishing to debt-finance and cross-subsidise the provision of infrastructure. Immigration may thus be construed as 'forcing the issue' but not causing it. A related point arises from the fact that immigrants are significant direct contributors to outer city growth.

Housing demand and house prices

Triple blow rocks housing industry

When the housing cycle goes into a trough, the one thing that keeps people in the game is the prospect that as sure as the industry slumps it booms. But there's been a depressing realisation during the latest deep decline in Australia's housing industry that the next peak won't be anywhere near the last one. The housing industry has changed fundamentally. Low inflation, low immigration levels and the diminishing cultural imperative of owning your own home have seen to that (*Sydney Morning Herald*, 2 December 1996)

Our grim future: it's an age old problem

The Housing Industry Association represents the sector which will be hit first and hardest [by declining population growth]. It now plans a major research project to examine the impact of immigration on the economy. The Business Council's Australia 2010 manifesto also underlined the role of immigration in Australia's development. It states 'as a sparsely populated nation, the size of our population must grow.' (*Sydney Morning Herald* 16 November 1996)

Since they make such a large contribution to population growth, it follows that Australians born overseas – both recent arrivals and longer term residents – significantly drive household formation and thus demand for housing (Figure 5.1). For many immigrants, in the early years after their arrival, this means the use of rental accommodation or else staying with friends and relatives (Paris 1993, p. 48). After a time, however, most immigrants aspire to home ownership with the same propensity as the Australian-born. In its report for the National Housing Strategy, Econsult (1992, p. 76) summed up the situation like this:

There is a substantial lag before many migrants are able to purchase a home, although the propensity to rent varies markedly between birthplace groups. Prior to five years residence, more than two-thirds of migrant households rent, compared with 28 per cent of Australian-born households. Of the total non-Australian born population, home ownership rates are only slightly less than for Australian-born households, and are higher than the average among migrants from India and Yugoslavia. Migrants from Vietnam are least likely to be home owners, which probably reflects the high proportion of relatively recent migrants.

Figure 5.1 Contribution of immigration to household growth, 1986-2001

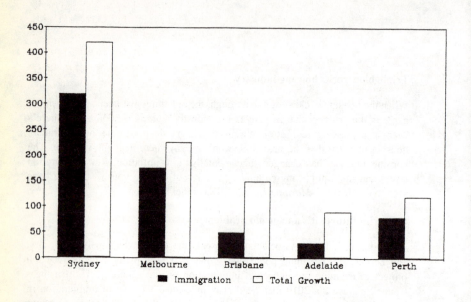

Source: Based on National Population Council (1990, p. 37)

Accurate forecasts of the demand for housing are critical to the housing industry for its operations. Prior to construction of urban subdivisions and housing, city planners must ensure that enough land is made available for development at the right time in the right places. Provision of infrastructure to development sites is a necessary precursor for this to occur. Because of the importance of the housing sector in the Australian economy, immigration-driven demand is considered critical by the housing industry. A drop in immigration is one factor behind housing industry recessions so the industry naturally supports continued high intakes.

Several studies have been conducted into immigration and housing matters. To obtain technical inputs to urban growth management, State governments constantly monitor population change and housing demand. Expectations about immigration are factored into forecasts. The situation was first comprehensively reviewed by Neilson Associates in 1982. More recent studies conducted by Sommerlad (1988), Murphy et al. (1990), National Population Council (1990), Junankar and Pope (1993) and Struik (1994) focussed especially on the relationships between recent immigrants and housing. These studies comprehensively summarised literature produced at the time they were made. This chapter focuses on the effects of immigration on housing prices and housing affordability since these have been of most public concern. Attention is also drawn to problems of housing stress experienced by particularly recent immigrants.

Immigration, house prices and housing affordability

Since immigration adds so significantly to demand for housing it has been associated with house price inflation in Australian cities – especially in Sydney which has the highest average housing prices in Australia and which attracts a disproportionate share of immigrants. To the extent that higher prices mean lower accessibility to housing for all new purchasers and renters of housing – and this will be the case unless incomes rise commensurately – then immigration may be further implicated in significant welfare declines for those forming households in cities where immigrants concentrate. This chapter first reviews some data on Australian housing prices and housing affordability and how they vary over time and across the set of Australian capital cities. The results of recent studies of factors associated with changes in house prices are then summarised so as to place immigration effects in the context of the full range of factors affecting prices. Research on variation in house prices and rents within cities, together with some other aspects of the relationship between immigration and housing, are also reviewed.

It is important to emphasise that in Australia access to good quality, well located housing, occupied by purchasers and renters, has been a plank of welfare policy for decades (National Housing Strategy 1991). Governments have supported high levels of home ownership in recognition of its iconic status as part of the great Australian dream. Some have argued that home ownership has also encouraged a more politically stable populace since those with mortgages to pay off and capital gains to accrue are less likely to mount the barricades in support of radical social change. In spite of the emphasis on home ownership, rental housing is still an important part of the stock but social (public) housing represents only five per cent of all housing units. Any threat to the capacity of Australians to achieve home ownership is therefore of major social and political significance.

Achieving home ownership requires that housing be affordable and affordability is an outcome of prices matched against the ability of buyers to pay. Prices include not simply the market price of houses and flats but also interest rates, since most buyers need to borrow substantial amounts of money to achieve ownership. Ability to pay refers primarily to income but may also be influenced by ownership of assets, including prior ownership of dwellings. Housing affordability has been falling in Australia for many years and this trend and the reasons behind it have been reviewed in a number of studies, most recently and comprehensively in a report supporting the National Housing Strategy (1991). A key finding of that study is that (p. 10):

> Housing costs consumed only 12.6 per cent of the incomes of Australian households in 1988, a relatively small proportion by world standards and up only slightly from 11.6 per cent in 1982. These national averages, however, disguise the fact that many Australian households have housing costs exceeding 25 to 30 per cent of their income. In 1988, for example [near the peak of the most recent immigration boom] just under 40 per cent of private renters paid over 25 per cent of their incomes on housing costs as did nearly 30 per cent of purchasers. For home purchasers and private renters, the proportion paying more than 25 per cent of income increased between 1982 and 1988.

Affordability varies over time with fluctuations in house prices and interest rates but the overall trend has been downwards since the late 1970s (Figure 5.2). For Australia as a whole, affordability has declined by half since 1979 but the capital cities were differently affected. The most striking figure is the low level of affordability in Sydney compared with the other capital cities. Sydney's disproportionate and increasing share of persons born overseas plausibly suggests that there is a causal relationship.

Figure 5.2a Housing affordability: ratio of deposit gap to annual household income (per cent), Australia and Sydney, Melbourne, Brisbane, 1979-1990

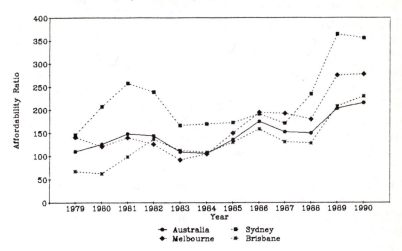

Source: Based on National Housing Strategy (1991, Table 3.1)

Figure 5.2b Housing affordability: ratio of deposit gap to annual household income (per cent), Australia and Adelaide, Perth, Hobart, Canberra, 1979-1990

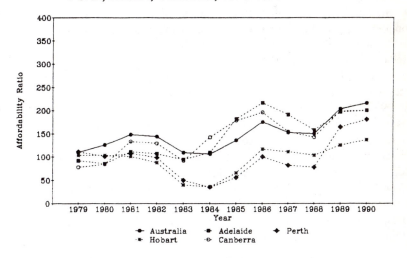

Source: Based on National Housing Strategy (1991, Table 3.1)

77

Immigration-fuelled population growth has certainly been linked with price inflation and declining affordability of housing both in the popular media and in a range of research studies (Murphy et al. 1990, Travers Morgan 1991a and b, Burnley and Murphy 1994, Maher 1994). While the coincidence of house price inflation and fluctuation in the immigration intake to Australian cities suggests causality there are other factors at work which drive both processes. In particular, a buoyant Australian economy both attracts increased numbers of immigrants and also fuels asset (including housing) price inflation due to high investor confidence. It is certainly logical that immigration-driven demand for housing will push up prices in the short run in cities where immigrants concentrate because the supply of housing is relatively inelastic. This is because it takes time for supply to adjust to increases in demand and there may thus be price inflation in the interim if demand increases cannot be accurately predicted so as to give sufficient lead time to city planners, infrastructure providers and home builders. In the longer run the coincidence of high immigrant numbers in the larger Australian cities implies, for reasons to be discussed below (and in the Technical Appendix to this chapter), real increases in the average prices of established housing. Theoretically, however, demand pressure should not in the long run inflate prices for new housing that is constructed at the edge of the city, which is where most new buyers locate. This is because the supply of land at the edge is theoretically limitless. More generally, the consensus of economists is that immigration has not fuelled inflation in all its aspects in Australia (Wooden et al. 1994, ch. 3)

A number of studies completed in the 1990s exhaustively analysed the costs of producing houses and sales prices and their relationship to levels and trends in immigration. The study by Travers Morgan (1991a) is the most comprehensive and authoritative of these. Travers Morgan assembled data on trends and levels in the prices of new and established housing in Sydney, Melbourne and Adelaide (Figures 5.3 and 5.4). The first two cities are the historically dominant settlement sites for immigrants, although as noted elsewhere in this book Sydney has opened up a large lead over Melbourne since the 1970s. Adelaide, a city with a much smaller population, was a significant destination for immigrants in the 1950s and 1960s but has been largely by-passed in recent years (for reasons which were discussed in Chapter 2). Perth and Brisbane, also key sites of contemporary settlement, might also have been included in the Travers Morgan study but it is unlikely that their inclusion would have much altered the tenor of results. Associations between time trends in housing prices, as well as differences in price levels as between the three cities, were analysed using econometric techniques. With reference to short and medium term changes the study concluded:

> In Sydney several variables help to explain variations, after allowing for income and interest rates, in house prices. Of these the one which most improved the

explanation was foreign migration into Australia. This had an impact elasticity of about 0.2. . . Another variable that improved goodness of fit (when not included with migration) was the real all ordinaries index [a measure of stock market performance] . . . Both foreign migrants and the all ordinaries index are likely to be correlated with a general sense of confidence in the Australian economy, which would drive expectations of capital gains in housing and hence lift house prices. *Most likely some combination of all three factors (migrants, equity prices and confidence), drives house prices.* (Travers Morgan 1991a, p. iv, emphasis added.)

No significant correlation between trends in immigration and shifts in house prices in Melbourne and Adelaide was found. This is not surprising since those cities, especially Adelaide, were much less attractive than Sydney to immigrants over the study period.

Travers Morgan (1991a) also analysed differences in house prices as between Sydney, Melbourne and Adelaide. They concluded:

Sydney's median house price is typically one-third higher than Melbourne's, which is in turn typically 15 per cent higher than Adelaide's [and, moreover]. . . prices have increased most in Sydney and least in Adelaide. (Travers Morgan 1991a, p. 128)

It is significant though that '[h]ouse price differentials are typically much greater at the top of the housing market and smaller at the bottom' (Travers Morgan 1991a, p. 128). It is at the low end of the market that first-home buyers concentrate and in welfare and political terms this group's interests are paramount. This finding is also consistent with the theoretical expectation regarding greater (theoretically infinite) supply elasticities in the outer city which was referred to above.

In its analysis of house price differences across the three cities the Travers Morgan study further concluded that 'differences in house prices are explained quite well by differences in city size, in house prices at the city boundaries, and by access costs' (Travers Morgan 1991a, p. 136). The larger the city the higher the price of established housing. If prices are higher at the edge of one city than at the edge of another this will have flow-on effects across the established city and result in price increases. Access costs here refer to costs of moving by private and public transport around a city. Australian cities tend still to be 'strong centred' so there is a price premium on land closer to the centre. Although immigration is not implicated directly in price differentials across the three cities, since immigrants influence a city's population level there is clearly a long-run indirect but strong association with the median prices of established housing. This partly assumes that cities favoured by immigrants retain their pre-immigrant populations. That is, that immigration is not balanced by losses from internal migration. In fact the evidence is, in relation to Sydney, that high immigration does correspond with higher net internal migration losses than are

Figure 5.3 Melbourne, Sydney and Adelaide: median house and apartment prices, 1974-1989 (comparison based on Melbourne equalling 100 per cent)

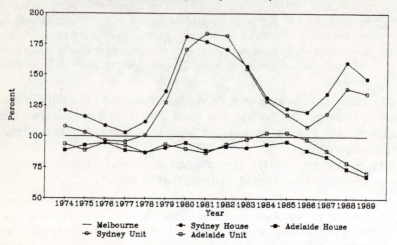

Source: Travers Morgan Pty Ltd (1991a)

Figure 5.4 Melbourne, Sydney and Adelaide: median price of new houses, 1984-1989

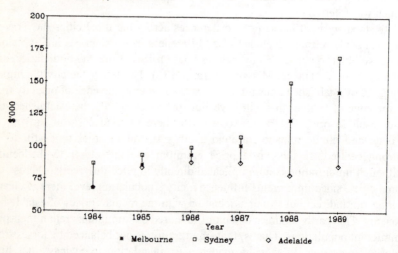

Source: Travers Morgan Pty Ltd (1991a)

observed in other cities (Murphy 1993). The precise relationship between immigration, population growth and house price inflation is therefore not so direct as theory might suggest.

Whatever the case may be regarding immigration's effects on long-run prices of housing, the fact remains that:

> Higher after-tax household incomes approximately compensate Melbourne households for higher housing costs compared with Adelaide. However, Sydney households must perceive non-monetary advantages . . . or substantial capital gains from housing because they have lower real incomes than Melbourne households. (Travers Morgan 1991a, p. 142)

Not only do immigrants disproportionately choose some Australian cities over others, but they also, of course, settle in varying concentrations across those cities. It may thus be inferred that in such localities housing prices and rent levels would be elevated as compared with localities less preferred by immigrants. The most comprehensive analysis of this topic was conducted by Burnley and Murphy (1994) who considered spatial variation in house prices in Sydney using demographic and price data for the period from 1976 to 1991. Using a variety of statistical approaches they came to a number of conclusions:

1. *While overseas migration was not positively associated with changes in median rents across Sydney in the period 1976-1981, it was moderately strongly associated with changes in median house prices.* There were no such associations in the 1981-1986 period. It is probable that the spatial association in the first period reflected growth in the late 1970s associated with the property boom, which in itself reflected investment trends. In the 1982-1985 period, when prices slumped in real terms, the volume of overseas immigration to Sydney as indicated by the duration of residence figures at the 1986 census was almost as great as that between 1976 and 1981. It is arguable that as immigrants tended to settle near to compatriots who had emigrated to Australia previously, a demand may have been created for owner-occupied housing near compatriots. Earlier established immigrants who previously rented may have wished to buy nearby, close to kin, friends, ethnic institutions and services. Owner occupancy in ethnic concentrations has been a distinctive feature of immigrant settlement in Australian cities (Burnley 1985) and this may have translated into increased local demand. The ability to pay associated with this also may have generated higher prices in some local areas. However, the strong immigration in the early 1980s did not have the same areal association with house price changes from 1981 to 1986.

2. *Overseas migration was not associated significantly with areal house price increases across Sydney between 1986 and 1991.* Given the large

intake of immigrants in Sydney in the late 1980s, equal almost to the post-war record, it had been hypothesised that immigration would have had a strong spatial association with median house price increases across the metropolis. This was not the case. Spatial trends in house prices varied considerably from those in the first two periods, reflecting, in all probability, changing residential preferences in general as well as factors linked with Sydney's further incorporation into the global economy.

3. *There was a slight association between overseas migration of earlier cohorts and median price changes between 1986 and 1991.* This modest association may have reflected the earlier arrivals having saved and later decided to buy

4. *While overseas migration was not associated with changes in median rents, it was moderately associated with areal increases in rents at the top end of the market in the 1981-1986 period.* Such associations reflect the migration of professionals and managerial workers and their families at a relatively greater rate than hitherto and their ability to rent in more salubrious areas and better housing. This association existed with persons from the United Kingdom and several countries in eastern Asia. Associations were significantly negative in the case of movements at the lower end of the market. There was no statistically significant association between price levels (purchase prices and rents), price inflation and where recent immigrants chose to settle within the city. The only exception to this was for rent levels in the higher brackets, which did have a weak positive correlation with immigrant settlement. This apparent paradox was explained by arguing that in localities of high immigrant demand, as soon as prices begin to rise, demand – from both recent immigrants and the rest of the population – shifts to nearby substitute locations, thus dampening inflation. The final outcome of these shifts would be increases in average price levels in a city but not in specific localities.

In truth, none of the findings from these studies of associations between immigration-driven demand for housing and prices are surprising since there is a well-developed economic theory of geographical or spatial variation in land and housing prices. The Technical Appendix to this chapter outlines that theory.

An important component of housing prices is the cost of supplying urban infrastructure to housing sites. Most new housing is constructed in the outer city so infrastructure costs – to the extent that they are charged to home buyers

Figure 5.5   Median house prices, Sydney 1986/1987

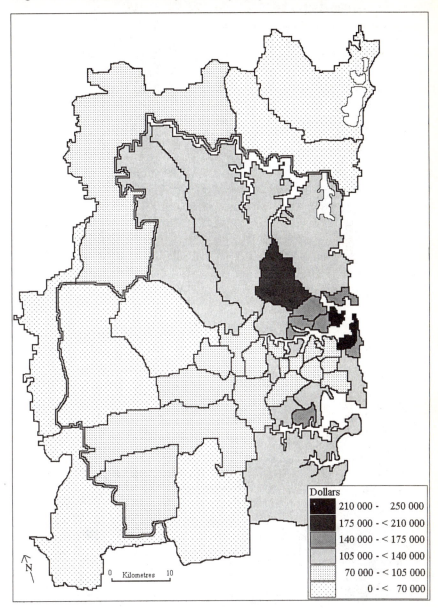

Dollars

■	210 000 - 250 000
	175 000 - < 210 000
	140 000 - < 175 000
	105 000 - < 140 000
	70 000 - < 105 000
	0 - < 70 000

0   Kilometres   10

Source: Based on Travers Morgan Pty Ltd (1991a)

Figure 5.6 Percentage changes in median house prices, Sydney 1986-1991

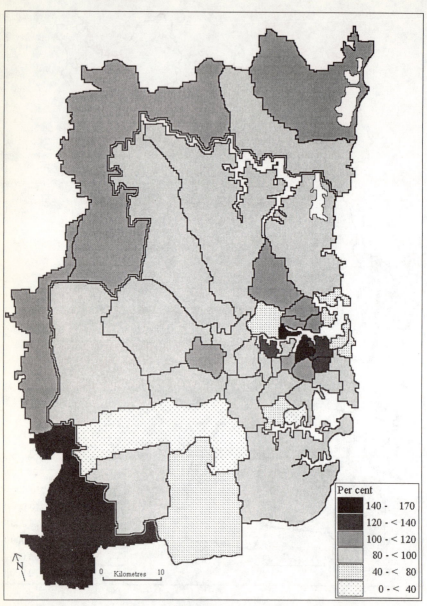

Per cent

■	140 - 170
■	120 - < 140
■	100 - < 120
■	80 - < 100
░	40 - < 80
░	0 - < 40

Source: Based on Travers Morgan Pty Ltd (1991a)

**Figure 5.7 Percentage changes in median housing rents, Sydney
1986-1991**

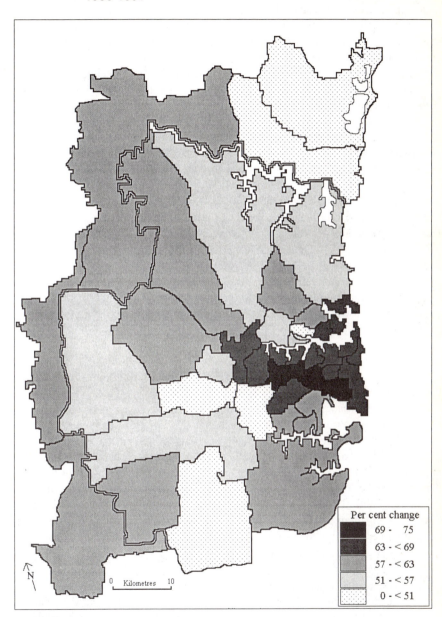

Per cent change
■	69 - 75
▨	63 - < 69
▦	57 - < 63
▨	51 - < 57
░	0 - < 51

0   Kilometres   10

N

Source: Commonwealth of Australia (1986-1991)

rather than passed back to land owners in the form of lower prices – will impact there. Any price inflation resulting from this source will flow through to higher housing prices in the established part of a city.

One of the arguments that has been put forward – specifically in relation to Sydney – is that immigration-driven housing demand is especially price-inflationary due to the higher costs of supplying infrastructure in that city. The argument goes that the supply of easily developed land at the edge of the city is less than around other cities, while at the same time the volume of new housing to be accommodated in Sydney is higher than elsewhere. Two sets of data assembled by Travers Morgan (1991b) shed some light on this matter.

Table 5.1 shows typical costs of producing housing allotments on the fringes of Sydney, Melbourne and Adelaide. There are clearly substantial differences in cost with the single major difference being the price of raw land. Both on-site and off-site infrastructure charges were also clearly highest in Sydney. While these figures lend support to the notion that immigrants settling in Sydney will directly or indirectly fuel house price inflation, there are caveats. Most notable is that off-site charges reflect price recovery policies of governments and there is evidence that in Sydney recovery levels are proportionately higher than elsewhere. Table 5.2 shows costs for dwelling construction in different categories in the same three cities. Building costs are much the same in Sydney and Melbourne but significantly lower in Adelaide. The authors contend that this reflects lower incomes in Adelaide rather than lower levels of housing demand.

Immigrants in housing markets

It is important to recognise that while immigrants may indeed collectively contribute to house price inflation, and that this may lead to reduced housing affordability – especially in a period when average real incomes are falling – these trends also affect immigrants themselves. This is especially the case with immigrants in the humanitarian category (primarily refugees) who for the most part have the lowest capacity to pay. They bring fewer resources with them to Australia and also tend to have the highest unemployment rates in the early years after their arrival. The National Population Council (1990, pp. 1-2) summarised the situation as follows:

> Migrant housing affordability is extremely low in Sydney; for some migrant categories dropping to less than half the level for the total population . . . In Melbourne migrant housing affordability is not as low as in Sydney but for some migrant families is below [an index number of] 100, the level at which families can just meet monthly repayments. A continuation of recent trends would put home ownership out of reach of nearly all migrants in the family stream in both Sydney and Melbourne.

It should be noted that these conclusions were reached at the peak of the late 1980s immigration surge and that the housing affordability situation has since improved markedly. Against this, unemployment among some groups of immigrants remains very high and must surely limit access to housing.

The National Housing Strategy report on the affordablity of Australian housing also drew attention to the problem of low-income groups in housing stress (National Housing Strategy 1991, pp. 26-7):

> Of concern ... are the 24 per cent of low-income units spending over one-quarter of income on housing; the 20 per cent that spend over 30 per cent; and the 8 per cent spending over 50 per cent. Indeed, those with low incomes are twice as likely as all income units to spend over 50 per cent of income on housing.

Table 5.1   Typical producer costs of land development in 1989-1990 (A$)

Item	Sydney	Melbourne	Adelaide
Land[1]	12,080	8,424	2,544
Land development			
on-site	14,300	12,700	10,700
off-site infrastructure	7,700	5,100	1,500
other charges	6,000	900	500
landscaping	500	350	500
fees	1,500 - 30,000	1,650 - 20,700	1,400
Total			14,600
Selling	3,900	2,700	1,560
Interest			
land	3,020	2,106	636
development	3,000	2,070	1,460
Margin	13,000	9,000	5,200
Total (price)	65,000	45,000	26,000

Notes: (1) Land computed as a residual after deducting costs from price.
All land costs computed above are lower than prices prevailing in 1989/90.
Source: Travers Morgan Pty Ltd (1991b)

Table 5.2 Summary of producer costs for selected dwelling types in Adelaide, Melbourne and Sydney, 1989-1990 (A$'000s).

Item	Cottage		Villa		Townhouse		Dual occupancy	
	contract	spec	Fringe	establish	fringe	establish	fringe	establish
Total costs (building and land)								
Sydney	115	123	106	178	124	186	106	168
Melbourne	95	103	97	161	120	178	95	163
Adelaide	65	71	71	118	95	137	0	0
Building (including interest and overheads)								
Sydney	50	57	83	120	107	144	65	87
Melbourne	50	57	81	114	109	143	65	86
Adelaide	40	46	62	85	88	113	0	0
Land								
Sydney	65	66	23	57	17	42	41	82
Melbourne	45	46	16	47	12	36	31	77
Adelaide	25	26	9	33	7	25	0	0

Notes: (1) Land cost at the urban fringe may include an economic rent. Differences due to rounding.
(2) Based on standardised construction costs for multi-unit dwellings.

Source: Travers Morgan Pty Ltd (1991b).

Regarding immigrants, the study noted (pp. 32-33):

> the likelihood of being in housing stress is higher for recently arrived migrants. Based on figures from the ABS 1988 *Housing Survey*, about 17 per cent of those who arrived after 1983 were in housing stress compared with 15 per cent for those who arrived between 1978 and 1982, and 11 per cent for those who arrived between 1973 and 1977. A recent report of the National Population Council (1990) shows that in 1986 a significant proportion of migrants were paying more than 25 per cent of their income on housing. For those in the rental market, the report identifies recent migrants from some countries (e.g. Lebanon, Vietnam, South America) as likely to have difficulty in meeting their housing commitments.

Public housing in Australia is, as noted above, a small but significant component of the housing stock. The demand for public housing substantially exceeds the stock and the situation has been worsening (Paris 1993). It is, however, difficult to obtain data from public housing authorities on the birthplace and recency of arrival of immigrants on the waiting lists. Such data may be considered politically sensitive since immigrants could be portrayed as competing with the locally born population for an important but scarce resource. The National Population Council (1990, p. 3) concluded:

> While at present migrants are not disproportionately utilising public housing, the evidence available indicates a growing need. Current levels of public housing investment will not meet this need, either in Sydney or Melbourne.

Conclusion

Immigration seems unquestionably to be associated – on theoretical and empirical grounds – with short and long term inflation in housing prices in Australian cities. In the short run the unpredictability of immigration levels means that supply constraints emerge in markets for housing allotments and dwellings. Price inflation during periods of high immigration is, however, also associated with the state of the national economy which simultaneously influences the propensity of people to migrate to Australia. Paths of causality are therefore blurred. In the long run, other things being equal, larger cities have higher prices for their established housing. Because immigration substantially drives population growth in Australia's largest cities, especially now in Sydney, it also logically drives price increases in the long run. The situation is exacerbated in Sydney because costs of land development at the edge of the city are higher than in other cities. The evidence is that affordability of housing is lower in Sydney and that people must either be prepared to spend a higher proportion of their income on housing or else compensate by living at higher densities or by relocating to other parts of Australia. It should be noted that in the long run, higher prices in Sydney result in greater asset accumulation, since capital gains are largely untaxed.

Although public housing represents a small part of the stock it is markedly under-supplied and most renters must fend for themselves in private markets. Waiting lists for public housing are long and lengthening. While immigration-driven household formation is clearly implicated in house price inflation, it must be recalled that immigrants themselves must face high prices. In the longer run immigrants too may adapt by choosing to shift to lower-cost locations. The tendency for these adaptations to happen will be strengthened by full cost-recovery for urban services and, as will be discussed in the next chapter, what economists refer to as *externality pricing* to deal with environmental deterioration.

Technical appendix

(based on Burnley and Murphy 1994, pp. 79-83)

An apparent contradiction is the comparatively strong association between annual trends in house prices, rents and annual rates of overseas migration on the one hand and lesser intercensal spatial associations between rent and price changes and the settlement patterns of recent immigrants within the cities. In fact these findings are not as contradictory as they may seem.

The resolution of the apparent contradiction lies in consideration of the standard economic model of spatial house prices. The elementary form of the model assumes a city with a single central node where all jobs and services are located. Because people seek access to the centre, and because near the centre the land available for housing is small, the interaction of higher demand and limited supply causes land values to be higher closer to the centre. Values fall away to the edge of the metropolitan region, and the rate of decrease is greatest near the centre (Figure 5.8). As aggregate regional demand for housing grows (to which overall population growth contributes strongly), the 'spatial price curve' shifts outwards. Thus the average price of established housing will increase over time (Figure 5.9). Prices on the edge for new housing will, however, remain relatively constant since supply at the edge of the city is elastic, that is, large relative to demand. As demand increases on the suburban edge, supply can accommodate it, and so prices remain stable. In the established city, however, unless population and housing densities increase, as demand increases so will prices. In sum, as a city's population grows so will average house prices and rent levels. Unless the real incomes of the city's population are also increasing at the same rate, the affordability of established housing will decrease.

Figure 5.8 Theoretical relationships between house prices/rents and distance from the core of a single-core city

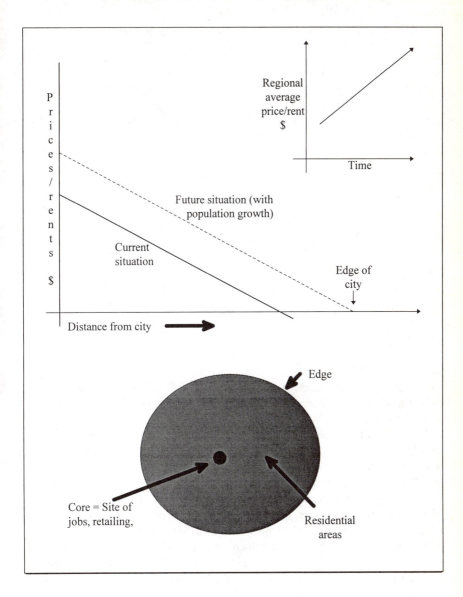

Source: Designed by the authors

Figure 5.9 Theoretical change in prices/rents with population growth in established parts and outer edges of a single-core city

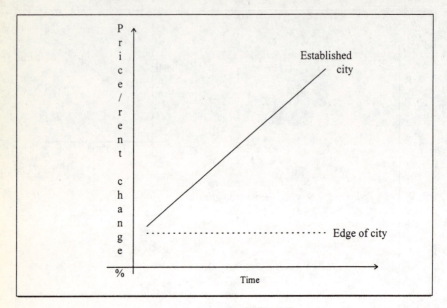

Source: Designed by the authors

The maps of rent and price changes (Figures 5.5-5.7) at least in part reflect these factors. It must be remembered though that, over time, Sydney has become a multi-nodal metropolis and that there are major distortions to concentric rent and price gradients caused by the harbour and beaches, given their high aesthetic and amenity value, and by the high income and amenity locations on the upper north shore, in Strathfield in the inner west, and around the Georges River estuary in the south.

So far, this discussion has been concerned with long-run trends. Over shorter periods, the supply of new housing at the edge of the city may be inelastic. An example is when providers of services such as water have not anticipated demand growth, so that increased rates of household formation lead to real price increases. In the established city, price inflation may be elevated to a higher level in the short term, since in the long run, households may purchase smaller housing units and live at higher densities.

Figure 5.10 shows the standard spatial price model plus sub-regions of the city where prices are elevated above the general trend. In these elevated price sub-regions, demand is in greater excess over supply compared with adjacent areas. In considering the formation and persistence of elevated prices, both short and long run perspectives are important. To start with, unless certain supply-side conditions prevail, these elevated prices will not persist over a long time. The supply-side conditions here refer to sub-regions in a city where the desirability of housing (or land for housing) is significantly higher than in adjacent areas. One such elevated price area may occur with 'gentrification' of inner city areas wherein 19th century terrace houses are occupied by households with higher incomes than prior residents, as has occurred in Paddington and Balmain in Sydney. Even in this case, when prices get to a certain level, gentrifiers may look further afield because proximity to the city centre is an important factor in their housing choice and not just the housing stock.

Figure 5.10 Selected relationships between house prices/rents and distance from the core of a single-core city, (a) with population growth between time 't' and time 't + n'; (b) with higher than expected prices locally; and (c) with restricted growth at the edge

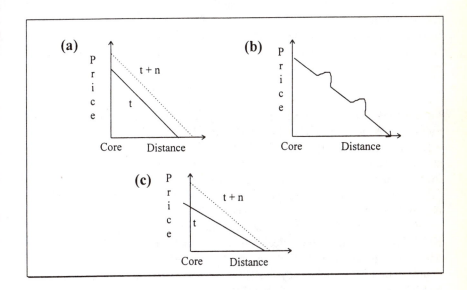

Source: Designed by the authors

It thus follows that, with the exception of cases where supply conditions are unique, any short-run tendency to regional elevated prices will be counteracted by demand shifting to areas adjacent to these. Such high prices clustering significantly above those predicted from the land rent/price model for their location will merge with the more general upward trend resulting from inflation and other factors. These higher-cost localities may never be more than marginally detectable, and certainly not on a long-term basis, although the trend in Ku-ring-gai SLA was indicative of a longer sequence with rents. Mostly, however, the elevated prices resulting from this kind of impact will disappear because there will be satisfactory alternatives to choose from. The result then will be that prices in elevated-price sub-regions of the metropolis will return to what is predicted by the spatial price model for the wider region in which the elevated price cluster is situated.

This finding by Burnley and Murphy (1994) of a less than strong association between patterns of immigrant settlement, housing prices and price inflation in areas of Sydney is thus quite predicable. *Indeed, from a theoretical perspective, any other finding would have been unexpected.* A number of further considerations can enhance conceptual understanding of the spatial price effects of immigrant settlement in a city like Sydney.

For instance, since recent migrants settle in a pattern which is concentrated relative to the host population, a potential for demand-driven price and rent inflation in sub-regions exists. There are two quite different situations in Sydney. First, many recent immigrants still settle in the inner and older middle ring suburbs. Secondly, many now settle in the outer parts of the established city close to where the bulk of new housing is constructed.

In the case of immigrants who settle in the established city, the tendency for local higher increases in rents or prices may be greater than on the edge of the metropolis if the process of diffusion of demand to adjacent areas is inhibited by a relative lack of supply of substitute housing. Here a significant finding of the study can be reconsidered: price and rent increases have been higher the closer the housing is to the centre. Rather than the situation indicated in Figure 5.10 (a) or (b), the circumstances are as described in Figure 5.10 (c). This implies that over time the highest-access locations have increased their comparative attractiveness, and this is almost certainly related to a regionalised but generalised gentrification effect (although such an association was not demonstrated across the whole metropolitan area). While this regionalised gentrification effect in Sydney has spread well beyond its diffusion centres of Paddington, Balmain, Glebe, Surry Hills, Birchgrove and Centennial Park, the continued preference of immigrants to settle in the inner parts of the city may well be adding to demand pressure. Spatially localised effects in the inner city may be lost in a *generalised effect* covering the areas affected by both gentrification and immigration in parts of the inner city. In some inner city localities in Sydney, as in Newtown, Marrickville and Dulwich Hill, a gentrification demand and immigrant settler demand may both have been present, especially in the late 1980s and early 1990s. Further work needs to be done to test the veracity of these inferences.

Near the edge of the city, the tendency for heightened rent and price increases will also exist, but to a much lesser extent due to the relatively elastic supply of land, bearing in mind that in western Sydney, many immigrants have taken up residence, at least in the first instance, in established houses and flats. Due to the elastic supply of land on the edge, immigrants would have little effect on prices, at the sub-regional scale.

Urban environment

There is a genuine challenge to the environment from population change. But it is important in the present state of knowledge to avoid the easy scapegoating of migrants by otherwise well-meaning people frustrated by the environmental problems they see … Australia should find and confront the real issues directly and not avoid them by taking premature refuge in assumed 'solutions' when there is a danger of committing both factual and moral blunders. (Withers 1991, p. 15)

On the environmental issues that are specific to Australia, there seems no case to restrict immigration in order to overcome identified environmental problems, which seem to be overstated in any event. These problems appear to be capable of solution, or at least of alleviation, by appropriate adjustments to environmental and resource management policies, including by giving emphasis to property rights and to proper pricing of resources. (Moore 1993, p. 39)

In line with the Premier, Mr Carr's views that Sydney is 'bursting at the seams', the NSW Government will take a proactive role in trying to cut the number of migrants settling in the city … 'I want Sydney interests to figure larger when the national immigration intakes are considered', Mr Carr said. 'It might suit Perth or Adelaide to have maximum intakes, but it's not in the interest of Australia's largest city'. (Humphries and Sharp 1995)

These quotations exemplify the flavour of debate about the relationship between population size, rates of population growth and environmental quality/ ecological sustainability that has been conducted at the national level and at the level of particular cities and regions within Australia. There is also, of course, the ultimately crucial debate at the global scale that represents the summation of damaging human practices in the myriad territorial units that comprise planet earth. At the national level there has been perennial consideration of the ecologically sustainable carrying capacity of the continent, with public discourse clamouring loudly over the past decade. Because of its major contribution to population growth the level of immigration has been an absolutely central aspect of this discourse. Views are typically polarised as to the impacts of population levels and rates of growth on environmental quality. At one extreme are those – the 'environmental determinists' – who argue that Australia is overpopulated already and that immigration should cease. The celebrated mammologist Tim Flannery (1995) exemplifies this viewpoint. He reckons that around 13 million people is the maximum. At the other extreme are those – the 'economic rationalists' – who see no limits to growth. Phil Ruthven (1995), the noted business analyst and economic commentator, reckons, for example, that the sky's the limit, with Australia's resource base having the capacity to support at least 200 million.

A 1991 issue of *Search*, the journal of the Australian and New Zealand Association for the Advancement of Science, illustrates how difficult it is to come to a common ground when people approach the debate from such radically different disciplinary perspectives. The editorial summary of the articles in that issue of the journal notes:

> environmental scientist John French [argued] that immigration policy has a fundamental place in any attempt to achieve sustainable development but his analysis [was] challenged by economist Lyuba Zarsky and the philosopher Chin Liew Ten. (*Search* 1991, p. 122)

Also in a dissenting vein is Jock Collins who, writing in the *Australian Left Review* (1991, p. 34), argued 'that the environmental case for shutting the gates [against immigration] is weak at best – shabby at worst'. But even environmental scientists such as Hollick (1994, p. 90) are not uniform in their positions:

> Australia has the capacity to support many more people than its current population . . . In the long term, its carrying capacity may be increased greatly by developing an economy and way of life with far lower resource demands and environmental impacts per capita. Most Australians would prefer to protect their way of life by restricting immigration but international pressures may make this impossible.

Clarke and Ng (1993, p. 73) express the mainstream economic-rationalist position as follows:

> If we have the right policies for the control of environmental disruption, then immigration certainly improves the average economic welfare of existing resident Australians.

The Australian Government has promoted informed discussion, notably through the work of the House of Representatives' Standing Committee for Long Term Strategies (1994) and of the National Population Council (1992). The work of the former has been reviewed by Mercer (1995 and 1994).

Problems of land degradation – particularly soil erosion, soil salination and reduced nutrient status of soils, and the eutrophication of rivers – along with ecosystem destruction and deforestation are unarguably much more significant in Australia than are urban environmental problems. But since these sorts of problems impact directly on so few people they are less likely to be politicised. In contrast, environmental problems in the metropolitan cities – especially air and water pollution – are prominent in public consciousness because of the numbers of people affected by them – or at least aware of them – on a daily basis. Not only do urban environmental problems affect people and the environment locally, air and water pollutants also contribute to global overload, for example greenhouse gases derived from motor vehicle exhausts. The engineering of ecologically sustainable urban development is thus an aspect of the broader global agenda. The Australian Urban and Regional Development Review *Green Cities* paper (1995) reviewed urban environmental issues in the context of ecologically sustainable development. Murphy et al. (1990) and Fincher (1991) have specifically addressed the relationship between such matters and immigration levels and settlement patterns in Australia.

No matter what the geographical scale of analysis, the key variables which influence environmental quality are population numbers, human behaviour and the characteristics of the environment itself. These variables interact to produce given levels of, and trends in, environmental quality. At the scale of urban settlements these variables take particular forms. But before considering the sources of, and possible solutions – including immigration control – to deteriorating urban environmental quality, we will first discuss the state of the environment in Australian cities. As has been argued in relation to other matters addressed in this book, only with such a context it is possible to properly characterise the impacts of immigration on urban environments.

Environmental quality in Australian cities

The final report of the National Population Council (1992, pp. xvii-xviii) into *Population Issues and Australia's Future* drew a number of conclusions about the state of Australia's urban environment. They are:

- Though knowledge remains all too limited, there is some significant evidence of negative influence of urban population growth on urban ecological integrity. It is recognised that important policy progress has been made in directly addressing some of these impacts. The Committee stresses the need for enhanced research and documentation of population and other impacts on urban environments.

- In regard to emissions of air pollutants in the major cities, there have been gains made in per capita emission reduction, but despite these there have been some net increases in emissions because of growth in population. Emissions of certain gases remain quite excessive and there are new localised air pollution problems associated with new settlement in less topographically and climatically favourable areas.

- In evaluating urban environmental issues the Committee focussed on Sydney and Perth as case studies, being two of the most important migrant-receiving cities. It appears that Sydney faces important physical and environmental constraints on its growth. Perth can accommodate substantial additional population at relatively low infrastructure costs, but it may be at some significant environmental costs.

- However, over the long term, immigration-induced direct pressure on the urban environment and on housing markets in Sydney and Melbourne will generate out-migration to presently less environmentally vulnerable and cheaper locations, like the north-east coast of New South Wales, south-east Queensland and the smaller state capital cities.

- In view of the emergence of a new population dispersal pattern beyond metropolitan boundaries, and given the pressures on major metropolitan environments, knowledge of the environmental outcomes in these new non-metropolitan areas of major population attraction is of great importance.

It is uncontestable that under present technological regimes and habits of human behaviour present patterns of urbanisation in Australian are producing unacceptable adverse impacts on the environments of towns and cities. Naturally, it is the larger cities where such problems are greatest. Although there are many types of urban environmental impacts the effects of air and water pollution are arguably the most significant from both human and non-human perspectives. In this regard, urban environmental problems in Australia are much the same – both in source and magnitude – as in other parts of the western industrialised world.

Each of the Australian States, whose governments are ultimately responsible for the management of urban development and its environmental impacts, has environmental protection agencies which monitor environmental trends and produce 'State of the Environment Reports'. Obtaining data that enables definitive conclusions about trends and spatial differences in environmental indicators seems a fair way off because relevant studies have not been undertaken; Birrell and Tonkin (1992) have also assembled some comparative data. There are also uncertainties about the effects of various pollutants. Not surprisingly, however, Sydney fares worse than other Australian cities in most respects. This is because Sydney is Australia's largest city; it is topographically constrained, which limits dispersal of polluted air; and it disposes much of waste water from new development in inland waterways as well as through ocean outfalls. In a less pronounced form the story is much the same in other Australian cities due to common behavioural patterns and regulatory arrangements.

The case of Sydney

Metropolitan Sydney exemplifies in their most pronounced forms the range of urban environmental problems in evidence in Australia and is now considered in a little more detail. Sydney is Australia's largest city, with a population approaching 4 million and a very low population density by world standards. It is also, of course, the most attractive city for immigrants so the association between immigration-driven population growth and deteriorating environmental quality is most pronounced, at least in public discourse. Air and water pollution constitute one set of concerns, traffic and aircraft noise, waste disposal and loss of agricultural land to housing are others.

The main sources of water pollution are domestic waste water – sewage and other household waste – and stormwater run-off from the land. Sydney's sewage is discharged via treatment works into water bodies. Provided that sufficient funds are spent on the latest technology – and in the past they have not been – such 'point sources' of pollution are in principle controllable; pollution is more or less able to be eliminated. Polluted run-off from the land is far more difficult to control and takes many forms. This matters in Sydney because rain can bucket down, turning the streets into rivers in an afternoon – especially in summer. From the built-up parts of the city, stormwater runs off into drains and collects oil, dog droppings, paper, plastic and all sorts of other rubbish. Apart from screening for solids such waste goes directly into water bodies. Agriculture at the edge of the city uses fertilisers and pesticides and these too get into water bodies.

Waste water and sewage goes into either the Pacific Ocean or the Hawkesbury-Nepean River on Sydney's western perimeter. While disposal to the ocean has adverse impacts on aquatic fauna and flora, it also threatens Sydney's beach culture. Many are the mornings after a storm when the beaches from Manly to Maroubra are declared too dirty to surf. The growing threat to water quality from sewage, and to a lesser but still significant extent stormwater drainage, became a major political issue in the 1970s. The State government committed millions of dollars to build deep-water ocean outfalls at North Head, Bondi and Malabar. These were (and are) the main sewage treatment works on the coast. Before the outfalls were commissioned, raw sewage – screened only for 'solids' – was dumped into the ocean at the base of sandstone cliffs. Sun and salt were left to kill bacteria and viruses and to dilute effluent in the water. Nothing is done to strip plant nutrients although this is less of a problem than inland, where algal blooms can result. In certain wind conditions undiluted sewage would drift into the beaches. As Sydney's population grew after the Second World War, conditions gradually worsened, with more effluent being discharged to the ocean. It included toxic effluent from factories which had blossomed in the industrial areas in the 1950s and 1960s. But it is not only people in Sydney who find pleasure at the beach – so increasingly do international tourists. The maintenance of high environmental quality is – and will increasingly be – crucial in sustaining the tourism expenditure which has come to be so important to Australia – and especially Sydney.

How effective the ocean outfalls are likely to be was seriously questioned by environmental activists in the mid-1980s. Under the headline 'Sydney's Toxic Waste Dump – The Pacific' Richard Gosden (1986, p. 18) put the situation thus:

> The Sydney Water Board is currently embarked on the first stage of a multi-million dollar publicity campaign aimed at convincing the public that the solution to the sewage pollution of beaches is in hand. The days of faecal lumps on the sand and chemical stinks in the waves are almost over. Television ads show surfers performing in pristine, sparkling waves. Double page colour spreads in magazines display bikini girls and high divers.

> The solution this wasted hyperbole is trying so desperately to sell is the extension of the ocean outfalls at Malabar, Bondi and North Head. Construction work has commenced on all three projects. The total cost in 1985 figures is put at $450 million and commissioning is expected for Malabar and Bondi in 1990/91 and North Head in 1992. The question is will it work and if it does, for whom.

Water quality at the main Sydney beaches was officially recognised to be poor in the monitoring period 1983 to 1987, with significant bacterial contamination. The deep-water outfalls commissioned in 1990-1991 have, at least according to official assessment, markedly alleviated this situation and beach users have noticed a major improvement in water quality. Yet sewage grease is still sometimes found on beaches and the level of grease in beach sands has not fallen to natural background levels. Pollution can still happen after heavy rains when treatment plants cannot cope with the volume of water. Stormwater pollution remains a serious problem, with over 200 outlets between Palm Beach and Cronulla. Environmentalists contest that levels of treatment are no higher and that while visible pollution has been reduced, especially on Bondi and Manly Beaches, damage to the aquatic environment persists – with fish toxicity being a real worry – while beaches in areas to the south, notably Cronulla, are now subjected to higher levels of pollution displaced from the coastline between Bondi and Maroubra.

The Hawkesbury-Nepean River supplies most of Sydney's drinking water. It is precious habitat for aquatic flora and fauna and a popular recreational resource. The river draws on a very large catchment – about 22,000 square kilometres – bounded by Goulburn to the south-west, Lithgow to the west of the Blue Mountains and the Broken Bay Plateau to the north between Hornsby and Gosford. The catchment is 65 per cent forested but there are extensive agricultural uses and increasing urban and industrial development.

Sydney's population growth is now almost entirely contained within the catchment of the Hawkesbury-Nepean River, which means that sewage and waste water will increasingly be disposed of in the river. For several years environmental activists have been vociferously drawing attention to worsening water quality, especially problems of viral and bacterial pollution. There is also the problem of plant nutrients – nitrogen and phosphorous – getting into the river from sewage and run-off from market gardens located on the river flood plain. These cause plant growth – notably of the toxic blue-green algae – and threaten eutrophication of the river with fish kills and strong odours of decaying vegetation.

The State government has responded by deferring large areas of land designated for urban development and implementing much higher technology effluent disposal. New housing at Rouse Hill in Sydney's north-west – an area which will be developed over 30 years and will ultimately yield 70,000 housing allotments – will, for example, have two water supplies, with separate plumbing. One will be potable water for household drinking, cooking and washing. The other will be recycled water for toilet flushing, car washing and garden watering. This is the first time such a recycling system has been available in Australia on anything but a trial scale. It will help reduce the demand for potable water – thus delaying the need for further dams – and will reduce the volume of waste water entering the Hawkesbury-Nepean river system. A new sewage treatment works is also being developed at Rouse Hill. De-watered sludge will be sold to fertiliser manufacturers and the treated water will be recycled or treated in wetlands and riffle zones being developed on site. As well as reducing the treatment plant's environmental impact, the wetlands/riffle-zone system will provide a sanctuary for birds and small wildlife and a recreation site for residents. These systems are expensive to construct and are arguably only possible because the land releases will attract predominantly upper- and middle-income purchasers. In the generally cheaper areas of the west and south-west such technology may mean higher costs to lower-income earners unless they compensate by buying smaller parcels of land and living at higher densities.

Sewage effluent has been the major source of pollutants that affect water quality in Sydney. In the 1980s levels of nutrients and plant growth measured by the Environment Protection Authority showed reductions. But excessive levels still exist in sections of the Hawkesbury-Nepean that receive discharges, with phosphorous, nitrogen, faecal coliforms and algae sometimes exceeding guidelines. The Environment Protection Authority believes that there is general downwards pressure on pollutant levels – especially improved water treatment with long-term effluent quality objectives expected to be achieved by 2000. Diffuse sources of water pollution continue to be a problem and the State Environment Protection Authority is shifting its focus to these. Environmental groups distrust the sanguine rhetoric of government and call for a ban on further urbanisation of the catchment. The problem is that there are as yet no clear alternatives. To ban development would lead to price increases and these would especially affect first home buyers who are struggling to get a foothold in the housing market. Politically, the State government is caught between the devil and the deep blue sea.

The main air pollutants in Sydney are lead compounds, nitrogen oxides, carbon monoxide, ozone, particulate matter, sulphur dioxide and other acid gases. Sources, levels and trends have been monitored by the Environment Protection Authority for many years. In its 1993 summation the Environment Protection Authority (NSW Environment Protection Authority 1993) presented the following information:

- Acid gases: Since 1980 levels have fallen and are well below long term health goals. Industry contributes 77%.

- Particulates (basically dust): Levels peaked in central and suburban Sydney in 1985 and have declined since then to below the National Health and Medical Research Council (NHMRC) annual average goal. 40% are from motor vehicles. Suburban levels are well below World Health Organisation guidelines; CBD levels are higher but still below.

- Nitrous Oxides: 80% from motor vehicles. Of this, heavy-duty, diesel powered vehicles account for 25%. Levels have exceeded NHMRC guidelines for years but introduction of three-way catalyst technology in new cars appears to have been effective. Trend has been down but not clear for future.

- Ozone and smog: In the 1970s, Sydney was Australia's most smog-bound capital. The situation has improved in recent years and the occurrence of photochemical smog has decreased. Future trends are unclear.

- Lead: Unleaded petrol was introduced in 1985 and lead levels have declined below the NHMRC standard. 60% of petrol sold is still leaded.

Sydney suffers from levels of air and water pollution similar to other large cities in the developed world. It is hard to disentangle fact from fiction with marked contrasts between the official and environmentalist discourses. Official reports suggest improved trends, while the Total Environment Centre (1992) referred to an:

> emerging air pollution crisis in western Sydney . . . Air protection in Western Sydney has a history of neglect and secrecy by all NSW Governments over the last two decades. In an educated and progressive society the public have a democratic right to be properly informed of matters that affect their health and lifestyle. With regard to air quality, this right has not yet been recognised by our politicians and bureaucrats.

Air pollution in Sydney is largely the product of motor vehicle exhausts. There are no electric power stations operating in the region and, while industry is a significant source of pollutants, Sydney is not a specialised heavy-industrial city. The problem is exacerbated by high levels of motor car ownership and the regional topography. High levels of car ownership, especially in the western and south-western areas of highest population growth, is linked – in a chicken and egg manner – to low residential densities. Although the 'quarter acre block', which gave Australian cities amongst the lowest densities in the western industrialised world, is for most home buyers long gone, the massive suburbanisation of the population which commenced in the 1950s has not abated. The outer areas of the city remain poorly served by public transport and numbers of jobs remain significantly lower than resident populations. Journeys to work are thus long and typically car borne. Cars which were initially luxuries have become necessities.

The situation is exacerbated by topography. Sydney is ringed by higher terrain: the southern highlands south of Campbelltown; the Blue Mountains west of Penrith and the Plateau country between Hornsby and Gosford. The effect is that that much of the region is poorly ventilated by prevailing winds. Instead of polluted air being dispersed away from the city, it tends to accumulate for long periods. Concentrations are especially high to the south-west, which is one of the major growth axes. From a global perspective even if wind clearance of pollutants was high, pollutants produced by Sydney's car-dependent population would be an environmental problem of considerable magnitude.

Tools for achieving ecologically sustainable cities

The ecological sustainability of Australian cities – indeed cities anywhere in the world – is a complex outcome of population levels, human behaviour, geographical context and urban form. Public policy has to influence one or all of these variables to be effective. The tools which may be deployed to that end are pricing of urban goods and services, regulation of environmentally destructive behaviour, and public education; in other words, the standard triad of tools discussed in any elementary textbook on resource economics. Their use to promote ecologically sustainable cities will now be reviewed so as to set the relationship between immigration-driven population growth and urban environmental quality in an appropriate context.

Controls over urban form

For the past 15 years or so Australian State governments have attempted to engineer higher residential population densities in the main cities (Troy 1995). This trend is popularly referred to as urban consolidation and involves the construction of residential flat buildings, townhouses, villa units and similar medium-density dwelling units. While most of the local political resistance to increased densities – and there has been a great deal of this – has come from the established inner and middle ring suburbs of cities, much of the density increase is actually coming in the new outer suburbs where the sizes of housing allotments are typically much lower than they used to be and a high percentage of medium density housing is being constructed there. There are several rationales for this trend to higher densities but a particularly important one is to reduce air pollution. The argument goes as follows (Newman and Kenworthy 1989). Australians are highly car-dependent at least partly because public transport – especially bus services – in the outer areas of cities is poorly developed. Bus services are poorly developed at least partly because population densities are too low to generate profits to private providers or acceptable levels of cost recovery for government services. This cycle of car dependency might thus in principle be breached if population densities were higher. This applies especially to new residential developments on the edge of the city where, in fact, most medium- and higher-density housing is now constructed.

Most of the effort to promote higher densities has involved land-use regulations and public education. These should however be regarded as necessary but not sufficient conditions for policy success. An important consideration here is that urban services have historically not been priced at levels needed for cost recovery. A good example of this is public commuter rail and bus transport in Sydney. A recent study by the New South Wales Government's Independent Regulatory and Pricing Tribunal (1996) concluded that while 'State Government funding of public transport's operating costs has declined, it still costs taxpayers some $361m per annum'. As part of its inquiry into taxation and financial policy impacts on urban settlement, the Australian Government's Industry Commission (now Productivity Commission) concluded that in Sydney cost recovery on water and sewerage services per housing allotment fell short by an average of $3900. Given an average cost of $25,000 per allotment, this implies that charges would have to increase by about 16 per cent in order to remove the estimated subsidy. Subsidies of this order exist in the other Australian cities. An inference from this sort of information is that population densities are lower than would have otherwise been the case. Full cost-recovery for urban services, or privatisation of services, which amounts to the same thing – and both are now inexorable trends – will arguably do more, as an unintended by-product, to increase residential densities over the next couple of decades than regulation and education could ever hope to achieve.

The pattern of expansion of cities into surrounding farmland and countryside also has significant implications for their ecological sustainability. There is a connection here with the question of population densities inasmuch as increases in density are theoretically capable of reducing the rates of fringe expansion; the more people we can accommodate within the confines of the existing city the less land need be converted to suburbs (NSW Department of Planning 1993). Realistically, though, eliminating lateral expansion of cities where demand for housing is increasing is a very long-term prospect and most growth in cities like Sydney will continue to be on the fringe. Re-direction of growth away from sensitive air sheds and water catchments, while desirable, is similarly unlikely to make a major short-run contribution to environmental management because people will simply not be prepared to live in localities which are inaccessible to jobs and services. It has to be understood that cities are very complex systems and have tremendous inertia to change. Like an ocean liner at full speed – only much more so – changing direction takes enormous effort over a sustained period of time. Controlling the environmental effects of lateral expansion must therefore rely on behavioural changes engineered over long periods of time, about which more below.

Regarding air pollution, apart from low residential densities, the separation of workplaces from homes is a key contributing factor (Cervero 1995). Getting a better balance between where people live and where they work has several potential benefits but, in the present context, to reduce the distances travelled would be to reduce air pollution. Like other aspects of urban form, patterns of work and housing location are largely the product of market forces responding to various prices, including, especially, prices of travel. Where those prices do not reflect the full (private and social) costs of the activities the tendency will be to over-consume. This is the root cause of long journeys to work. Like other aspects of urban form, things cannot be changed overnight. Like other aspects of urban form, regulation and education will only go so far in achieving change, and pricing must be accepted as an integral part of the solution.

Successions of (State government produced) metropolitan planning strategies have reiterated concern about imbalance between jobs and housing and the long journeys to work which result. While over the years large numbers of jobs have been created within, and have relocated to, the outer city, the imbalance compared to residential populations remains large and has worsened (see Manning 1978; Alexander, 1981; NSW Department of Urban Affairs and Planning 1996). The current situation in Sydney, Australia's largest city, was summed up by the New South Wales Government in 1991:

> Jobs are not spread evenly within Sydney. Eastern Sydney has about one third of the Sydney Region labour force but more than half of the jobs. Between 1981 and 1990 the resident labour force in the Western Suburbs grew by nearly one third, but the number of jobs grew by less than one fifth. With the exception of commercial and retail growth in centres such as Parramatta, Liverpool, Fairfield and Penrith, and the development of a number of business parks, there has been

little movement of jobs to outer suburbs. At the same time, the growth of outer residential areas is increasing the distance between where people work and where they live.

More detail is to be found in results from the New South Wales Department of Transport (1996) household travel survey, which show that:

> trips to work were longest in the outer fringe areas such as Gosford, the Blue Mountains, outer south western Sydney and Fairfield-Liverpool. There was a marked increase in travel time in 1991 compared with 1981 in most of these areas, especially in Gosford and Wyong. As population grew faster than employment opportunities in these areas residents had to travel further to work. (p.10)

Controls over behaviour

From a policy viewpoint, the most direct and effective means of maintaining ecologically sustainable cities is to dampen behaviour which works against sustainability. If we want lower air pollution, for example, we must drive our cars less. The most direct method of achieving this objective is to make cars more expensive to drive and thus reduce levels of use. Air pollution is a social cost or *negative externality* in economic jargon. Its existence means that people are not being required to take the pollution they generate into account when they make decisions to drive. Were they required to do so they would drive less, with the result that emissions would be reduced to sustainable levels. Price increases may be most effectively achieved by higher taxes on fuel. An issue that must be contended with here is that what are known as price elasticities of demand for petrol are low. That is to say, modest price increases do not have much of an impact on demand for petrol. This derives from the fact that many people are trapped into car dependence due to the unavailability of effective substitutes in public transportation. The same reasoning applies to the case of water pollution. If we want, for example, effluent free of plant nutrients (nitrogen and phosphorous compounds) so as to prevent accelerated eutrophication of enclosed water bodies then we must discourage people from using products such as detergents and fertilisers which contain them. Again, 'externality' pricing imposed by regulation is the most direct and effective means of achieving the objective. It is worth reiterating, before moving on, that externality pricing will result in behaviour shifts which in turn will produce shifts in urban form: increased densities, reduced rates of lateral expansion and closer relationships between where people live and where they work. Those shifts will in the long term compensate people for inconvenience incurred by the shifts which they will need to make in their behaviour.

Controls over population

A [New South Wales] Premier's Department briefing paper, prepared for Mr Carr, portrays a Sydney where, on current projections, the quality of life has been much reduced. The gloomy scenario has fuelled Mr Carr's enthusiasm for population control in Sydney on economic and environmental grounds, prompting remarks such as his weekend urging of disincentives for immigrants to settle in the city. (David Humphries, *Sydney Morning Herald*, 22 May 1995)

The chairwoman of the Ethnic Communities Council of NSW, Mrs Angela Chan, said Mr Carr's proposal [to reduce immigration so as to control environmental deterioration in Sydney] ignored the importance of family reunion as a motive for migrating to Australia. 'There was no way migrants or anyone else could be forced to live in regional areas', she said. When told yesterday that the [State political] Opposition was accusing him of having offended ethnic groups Mr Carr said: 'Nobody could be offended by it. What I'm talking about is getting sensible planning policies that protect Sydney'. (*Sydney Morning Herald*, 24 May 1995)

NSW Premier Mr Carr's call for a curb on immigration to ease Sydney's population pressures put the city's claim to be a regional headquarters for multinationals in the Asia Pacific at risk, the [then] Minister for Immigration, Senator Bolkus, said yesterday. In a carefully worded rebuke to the Premier, Senator Bolkus noted that of the 130 regional headquarters established in Australia since September 1993, investing $2.3 billion in the economy and creating 2000 jobs, 70 per cent had gone to Sydney. 'In this era of globalisation, we can't say to the rest of the world we want your money but we don't want you.' (Catherine Armitage, *Sydney Morning Herald*, 22 May 1995)

If human behaviour and urban form remain constant then slowing rates of population growth in cities, even curtailing growth completely, will contribute to their ecological sustainability. But questions of how to achieve such objectives arise. So to do questions of the relative effectiveness of population control, compared with controls over urban form and environmentally damaging behaviour.

The particular attraction of population control in Australia, and especially in cities like Sydney, which appears to have the most deteriorated environment, is that growth is strongly driven by immigration. Compared with the movement of people within Australia and natural increase through the excess of births over deaths, controls over immigration are relatively straightforward. Technically the Australian government could stop immigration overnight – although of course political realities are such that this is implausible. Controls over natural increase and internal migration are nevertheless far less feasible.

From a purely technical viewpoint, reducing immigration to achieve sustainable cities is a second best option (Tolley and Crihfield 1987). First of all, if immigration is halted this will not stop population growth overnight. This is partly because any population holds the potential to grow from natural increase. In the case of Sydney, it has been noted that when population growth from immigration is high more people leave to live in other parts of Australia (Murphy 1993). Conversely, when immigration is low the outflow of people from Sydney declines. The implication of this relationship is that if immigration is reduced the effect on Sydney's population growth will be much less than proportional. A second reason why controls over population growth are a second best option for dealing with environmental problems is that such a strategy will only defer attacks on the more fundamental issue of environmentally damaging behaviour.

Summation

Unquestionably there are significant environmental problems in Australian cities and, other things being equal, the larger the population of a city the greater will be the pressures on the natural environment. But population levels and rates of growth are merely part of a complex set of forces influencing environmental quality, and control of population is not self-evidently the sole or the most effective way to go. In relation to the broader environment–population debate, Clarke and Ng (1993, p. 272) summarise the situation as follows:

> Provided resource and environmental externalities are dealt with by efficient pricing policies, it is contended that existing people benefit from population increase whether it derives from immigration or natural increase . . . While some might contend that these pre-conditions are rather daunting (in particular efficient pricing of all resources), the general viewpoint seems important because it shifts attention to pricing policies, over which we as a community have control, rather than focusing on abstract and speculative concerns over what constitutes a desirable population.

Constraints on achieving ecologically sustainable cities

The technical principles of achieving ecologically sustainable cities are thus well established. One of the problems in implementing these principles is, however, that urban managers and politicians typically lack economic literacy as opposed to physical planning and civil engineering skills. They thus typically conceive of urban environmental management, and urban planning generally, as an exercise in setting regulations, in public education, and in improved coordination between State and Local government agencies. While those approaches are essential, market forces strongly limit their effectiveness while simultaneously pointing the way to the most direct and effective means for policy implementation.

The less tractable constraints on achieving ecologically sustainable cities are political. Immigrant, environmentalist and social justice interests have conflicting agendas which hamstring action in support of the environment. Because such a high percentage of Australia's population was born overseas there is quite naturally a vital interest in permitting substantial family reunion migration. The overseas born will for the most part weight this concern more heavily than the improvement of environmental quality. Part of the reason for this is that immigrants, like all people, may find it difficult to understand the cumulative effect of what they see as their own only marginally damaging actions. After all, how could the little bit of pollution created by the use of your own car be such a problem. This is the classical 'commons' problem so eloquently articulated in Garret Hardin's famous essay (1968).

Environmentalists are also inevitably biased in their own ways. Unless they were themselves born overseas, or are related to recent immigrants, it is reasonable to assume that they would find it difficult to identify with the social imperatives which drive family reunion. Similarly, where they themselves have jobs, environmentalists may find it difficult to personally relate to those who regard population and economic growth, with their corollary – under present laws and practices – of environmental degradation, as having priority.

The social justice lobby in its turn may concede immigrant and environmentalist viewpoints yet reject effective means to maintain ecological sustainability. Theirs is an ideological reaction, based only partly on facts, against the use of pricing as a tool for environmental management. As far as it goes this perspective is valid. The case of leaded versus unleaded petrol is illustrative. To encourage owners to rapidly retire the stock of cars which burn leaded petrol would require a much larger differential in petrol prices than exists now. But it is older cars which burn leaded petrol and these are predominantly owned by poorer people. Another example concerns tolls on urban freeways in Sydney. Equity, it is claimed, demands that tolls be removed since it is longer-distance commuters from the outer suburbs of Sydney who use them most and such people are assumed to be poorer than average. There is also a matter of inter-generational equity, one of the principles of ecologically sustainable development. Those who live in the established parts of the city have available for their use roads which they have not had to pay for. Yet road pricing to reflect environmental damage is the only logical way to reduce environmentally deleterious behaviour.

Externality pricing, and more generally cost-recovery pricing for urban infrastructure, are clearly the linchpins of ecologically sustainable cities. Properly conceptualised and implemented, their use is capable of defusing conflicting social justice, environmentalist and ethnic agenda. Equity effects need to be and can be identified. Where appropriate those who are adversely affected will need to be compensated; more on this below. Externality pricing will, of course, satisfy environmentalists: ecological sustainability will be rapidly and efficiently achieved – as part of this process urban form and city size will adapt to more sustainable forms. City planners must anticipate and accentuate such shifts through regulation and coordination of the actors involved in urban development. Immigrants should also be content in so far as immigration need not be curtailed or, if it is, as a complementary measure, reductions can be modest. But neither immigrants nor environmentalists will be happy, any more than the rest of the population, with the shifts in behaviour which cost-recovery pricing must engender. They too will be differentially affected by pricing. To the extent that immigrants and environmentalists are poor – though just how poor is an issue – then compensation eases or eliminates the burden. If they are not poor then the challenge is for them to accept, like all of us, enforced shifts in behaviour for the common good.

Equity impacts need not then be unmanageable if implemented properly over reasonable periods of time. The *Interim Report* of the Economic Planning and Advisory Council's Task Force on Private Infrastructure (May 1995) discusses the distributional impacts of user pays and, by extension, externality pricing. There are indirect and direct means to compensate those least able to absorb increased costs of living resulting from measures to protect the environment.

Two categories of indirect means of compensation may be identified. First, as higher levels of resource costs for infrastructure provision are recovered, governments may be able to decrease taxes or to increase spending elsewhere. A second option arises when reductions in charges for business users (e.g. of water), consequent upon the removal of cross subsidies, may be partly passed on to consumers in the form of lower prices.

Three direct means of compensation may be deployed by governments when people are adversely affected by externality pricing, and cost recovery pricing generally. First, direct payments may be made to individuals designated through means testing. Secondly, payments, equal to the differences between the full costs of service provision and the subsidised price which governments deem appropriate for designated groups, may be made to service providers. A third compensatory option is for public sector providers to reduce the required rate of return on their assets, thereby reducing government dividend requirements.

Conclusion

Human practices in Australian cities are at least as environmentally damaging as anywhere in the western industrialised world. Fundamental changes will need to be engineered over the next few decades if ecologically sustainable cities are to be achieved. From a policy viewpoint the 'first best' approach to achieving sustainable cities is to modify behaviour through a combination of pricing, regulation and education. Application of this approach will indirectly limit population growth as people choose to live in cheaper localities or places where their choices are less constrained. Application of first best approaches nationally will limit the attractiveness of Australia for immigrants. Controlling immigration in order to control population growth in order to control environmental degradation, is a 'second best' policy option, the deployment of which is politically fraught. Lowered levels of immigration may, however, be seen as providing 'breathing' space while more effective means are implemented.

As a coda to this chapter, the issues raised in a *Sydney Morning Herald* article of 16 November 1996 make interesting reading. The authors, Paul Cleary and Diane Stott, start their piece by suggesting:

> the catchcry of 'populate or perish' has lost its impact as Australia approaches the next century. The Coalition is grappling with the immigration debate, and there are growing doubts that a low population can deliver economic prosperity.

They continue:

> A frightening future awaits Australia in the 21st century as fears of high immigration and related population growth persist in determining government policy. Australia is heading for a small, stable but rapidly aging population within a generation. And this threatens to undermine future economic growth and integration with the Asia-Pacific region. The engine for Australia's economic growth for half a century will have seized up. [In the face of high population growth rates in Asia] Australia's low population growth presents a huge risk to both economic and security interests.

Who would be a politician!

Urban labour markets

The 1990s have seen a resurgence in the long-standing debate over relationships between immigration and the labour market. Since the beginning of large-scale immigration programs in the 1950s, these relationships have tended to become controversial only at times of economic recession and high levels of domestic unemployment. The immigration-employment issue in the 1990s, however, has been given added impetus by a revived debate over economic, social and environmental problems in Australia's largest cities, which continue to suburbanise. Earlier chapters in this book show the heavy concentration of Australia's overseas-born population in the capital cities, especially Sydney and Melbourne. Not only have migrants concentrated here but there are strong tendencies for certain overseas-born groups to concentrate in inner and outer suburban places which have consistently exhibited among the highest levels of urban unemployment.

Unfortunately, debate over the impact of immigration on employment in the cities has been clouded by four things: first, the highly uneven levels of unemployment throughout Australia since the early 1980s and debates about how these should be addressed by public policy; secondly, debate about important changes in the sources of immigrants to Australia after 1980; thirdly, related arguments about benefits and costs to Australia of multiculturalism; and finally, debate over Australia's relatively high rate of population growth by OECD standards and its impact on the urban biophysical environment including air and water quality. A review of recent research into relationships between immigration and Australia's urban labour markets, however, suggests three things:

1. Connections between rates of immigration, the nature of migration flows and the labour market in cities are often misunderstood, are difficult to establish and have attracted little systematic research to date.

Historical evidence about connections between immigration and employment at the national level are commonly drawn upon in debate but often misunderstood or misrepresented at the scale of the cities and other Australian regions. Indeed, in a major review of the national labour market experiences of immigrants, Wooden (1994b, p. 279) concludes that 'there has been no analysis of how immigrant labour-market experience varies across different regions within Australia'.

2. In an Australian economy which has been globalising and rapidly restructuring, the context for understanding immigration and labour markets in the large cities is fundamentally different in the 1990s than it was in the 1960s. Much of the debate draws on historical evidence and fails to take account of the new global framework for understanding immigration and recent population movements, for example in the Asia-Pacific Region.

3. Although it is commonly overlooked, people's detailed labour market experiences are locally determined (Peck 1996). This is no less the case in the age of the global economy and occurs despite the high degree of labour mobility present in Australia. To open a more informed debate on connections between immigration and labour markets in the largest cities, we need to know how labour markets work in particular places. Information about this is surprisingly scarce.

Public perceptions about immigration and unemployment

Since the early 1980s, then, public opinion on connections between immigration and metropolitan labour markets has been shaped largely by perceptions and political rhetoric rather than by evidence. During Australia's long boom of industrial growth between 1950 and the early 1970s, there was little public opposition to high levels of immigration, most of which targeted the capital cities. This reflected, in part, bipartisan political support for the view that net economic benefits flowed to Australia from both the post-war immigration program and continued urbanisation of the population.

There was little or no opposition, for example, from the Australian trade union movement. Migrants did not undermine levels of union membership, for example by contributing to growth of secondary labour markets in the cities; nor did they depress wages either in general or in particular sectors of the economy such as manufacturing, where migrants became concentrated (Quinlan and Lever-Tracy 1990, p. 175). Overall, Australia did not seek to develop a 'guest worker' scheme such as occurred in many Western European countries. Permanent settlers were sought and, in theory at least, migrants were encouraged to join trade unions and share the conditions of other workers (Lack and Templeton 1995, p. 81). This did not prevent increasing segmentation of the labour markets in the large cities, 'the key axes being country of birth and gender' (Collins 1988, p. 78). Migrants of non English-speaking background (NESB) became concentrated in manufacturing, building and construction, although these were sectors which recorded steady growth between 1950 and the mid 1970s.

Since the early 1980s, however, Australia's national unemployment rates have not fallen below 6 per cent while peaking at over 10 per cent in 1983 and close to 11 per cent in 1992 (Figure 7.1). Under these circumstances, opinions have surfaced more regularly that newly-arrived migrants might be competing with local people for scarce jobs or contributing to growing pools of city workers with little choice but to accept increasingly casualised jobs in sweatshops or at home. According to Maddock (1993, p. 109), since the early 1980s:

> the public have been convinced (despite the weight of evidence) that migrants add to the size of the unemployment problem and politicians have responded by reducing intake quotas.

Fears have also been expressed, especially in the media, about the assumed consequences of high unemployment rates for relations between ethnic groups within the largest cities. Significant migration intakes, especially into Sydney and Melbourne, from Middle Eastern countries and from East and South-East Asia over the period of economic restructuring since 1980, make these immigrants more visible targets for such opinions. Yet a survey conducted in outer suburban Melbourne in 1992, an area with both a sharply rising proportion of NESB residents and high levels of unemployment, suggested that these fears were unfounded (Markus 1993, p. 37). There was little evidence that Australian-born people blamed immigrants for locally high unemployment levels and no specific antagonism was expressed about particular groups. Nearly half the sample, however, thought immigration levels were too high given Australia's economic circumstances. By June 1996, an AGB-McNair poll found that two-thirds of people in a nationwide sample thought levels of immigration were too high and three-quarters of these gave levels of unemployment as the main reason for their opinion (Millett 1996, p. 6).

Figure 7.1 Unemployment rates in Australia, 1967-1994

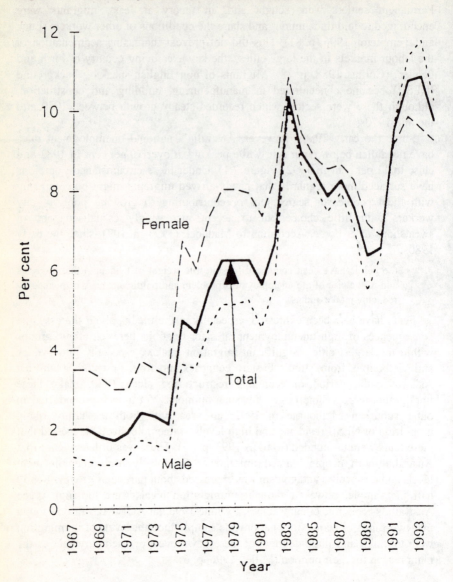

Source: Rich, D.C. (1995)

Immigration and employment: a perspective

Despite considerable evidence about connections between immigration, employment and unemployment at the national scale (see Wooden 1994b) there is little detailed analysis of either specific cities or the differential experiences of immigrants, especially people from non English-speaking backgrounds, in the parts of the largest cities where they have become concentrated. Since the 1980s, there has been substantial restructuring of the economies in the largest cities and dramatic de-industrialisation of their labour forces (Murphy and Watson 1994). While governments of all political persuasions have been committed to neo-liberal economic policies – including the rhetoric of 'deregulation' – to internationalise the economy (O'Neill and Fagan 1995), the earlier bipartisan political support for relatively high levels of immigration has fractured in the more difficult economic climate. The debate over immigration became even more vigorous with the return to Federal government of the conservative Liberal-National Coalition in 1996 and sharp differences of opinion emerging across the political spectrum about the costs and benefits of the immigration policies of the previous Labor Government. Again, however, these recent debates about immigration have been clouded by, and often confused with, political argument about multiculturalism.

The conventional wisdom about net economic benefits flowing to Australian society from immigration has rested on three arguments:

1. Immigration contributes to continued growth of the domestic market. This was the basis on which Australian manufacturing grew after 1950 against the tide of international industrial concentration in the northern hemisphere. In the 1980s and 1990s, this argument rests on the role of migration in keeping up demand for both manufactured goods and an expanding range of services, the provision of which now employs the vast majority of the Australian labour force. Wooden (1994a, p. 146) concludes that 'the impact of immigration on demand has historically more than compensated for impacts of the consequent expansion in labour supply'.

2. Immigration provides a labour force for manufacturing in the growing industrial cities and can help fill particular skill shortages. During the long boom, immigrants included workers with specific skills but also a large semi-skilled or unskilled factory labour force which provided a foundation for the cliche (not always accurate) that migrants, especially NESB settlers, filled blue-collar jobs that 'Australians would not do'. Overseas migrants made the most significant impact on the growth of Australia's labour force between 1947 and 1961 when some 73 per cent

of its growth was attributable to immigration (Tait and Gibson 1987, p. 5). During the last 20 years, however, the rising participation rate of women has made a much bigger impact on the growth of metropolitan labour markets than continued receipt of overseas migrants (Young 1988, p. 228). In these recent years, according to Fisher (1981, p. 8) and Clarke and Ng (1991), immigrants still create more jobs than they take up because of: first, their contribution to stimulating aggregate demand; secondly, their provision of new skills; and, thirdly, the well-known tendency of (some) immigrant groups to establish new small business and take on workers (Collins et al. 1995).

3. Some economic analysts have argued that immigration makes a net economic contribution by slowing down the rising average age of the Australian population, a major demographic phenomenon over the last 20 years. Growth of population through migration might thus help to offset the 'greying' process which means relatively more PAYE tax-paying members of society to support the increasing demands on government services from an older population (see Tu 1991). Yet demographers such as Young (1988) have refuted these claims, and in a survey of demographic evidence Hugo (1994, p. 63) concludes that only with unprecedented increases in the annual intake could immigration make more than a small impact on this ageing process. In any case, the problems for Australian cities of this population ageing process have often been asserted rather than established through analysis. An increasingly youthful population could add to environmental and labour market pressures especially in suburban locations.

The employment experiences of immigrants are crucial in all three of these arguments. A major problem with economic analyses of immigration, however, is that they are inevitably carried out at highly aggregate levels with historical data. Hence, it is difficult for them to be sensitive to the sharply changed circumstances of social and economic life in Australian cities of the 1990s compared with experiences of the 1960s. In these cities, labour market experiences of immigrants have depended strongly on their time of arrival in Australia, the changing experiences of those economic sectors in which overseas-born workers have become concentrated, and factors specific to those particular parts of the cities in which migrants have congregated.

Migrants in the cities have continued to concentrate in particular industries and occupation groups. Table 7.1 uses Sydney as an example and shows the concentration of NESB groups in blue-collar jobs, especially in manufacturing and the trades. These occupations held some 27 per cent of Australian-born workers at the 1991 census compared with 48 per cent of Lebanese-born, 51 per cent of Italian-born, 54 per cent of Vietnamese-born, 57 per cent of Greek-born and 63 per cent of those from the former Yugoslavia. In Sydney, migrants from Greece, Italy, Yugoslavia and the Asia-Pacific region remained under-represented among service workers (now the fastest-growing employment group), professionals and managers. Migrants from Northern European countries, especially the United Kingdom and Ireland, had a sectoral and occupational profile similar to Australian-born workers and were found throughout service industries and in managerial or professional occupations. Self-employment was highest among long-established migrant groups, especially people from Greece and Italy.

In a survey of recent research, Wooden (1994b, p. 247) shows that NESB migrants remain relatively highly concentrated in blue-collar jobs, although for NESB males there is some evidence of upward occupational mobility – an

Table 7.1 Occupation by birthplace, Sydney 1991 (per cent in category)

	Aust-ralian born	UK/ Eire	Italy	Greece	former Yugo-slavia	Lebanon	Viet-nam
Manager/ administrator	11.1	14.0	11.3	9.3	5.1	9.6	4.1
Professional	15.1	15.3	5.4	3.8	5.1	5.5	7.7
Para-professional	7.2	8.0	2.5	1.4	3.4	2.3	3.8
Clerks	19.4	17.8	8.9	5.5	8.3	9.2	12.9
Sales and personal services	14.7	12.7	11.1	13.4	6.8	13.7	7.8
Tradespersons	12.3	12.7	21.9	15.9	22.8	17.3	14.1
Machine operators/drivers	5.4	5.1	9.4	11.5	13.2	12.2	18.5
Labourers and related	9.1	9.1	19.5	29.2	26.6	18.9	21.5
Other	5.7	5.1	9.9	10.1	8.7	11.4	9.5
Total	100.0	100.0	100.0	100.0	100.0	100.0	100.0

Source: Australian Bureau of Statistics (1991b)

'urban escalator' – with increasing length of residence. Lack and Templeton (1995, p. 82), however, describe this proposition as a myth. Campbell et al. (1991) examined the labour market experiences between 1970 and 1988 of a sample of immigrant workers employed in Melbourne's manufacturing sector. Only one-fifth of these workers had experience of manufacturing work before their arrival in Australia. Male immigrants concentrated in basic metal industries, metal fabrication and motor vehicle production while women quickly became concentrated in textiles, clothing and footwear production. Their study also discovered that among the groups of NESB immigrants surveyed less than one-fifth showed any significant occupational mobility over time. The major change was the entry of some workers into small business, sometimes in manufacturing but mostly in the service sector (see Collins et al. 1995). The most recently arrived group in the study, the Vietnamese-born, were even more concentrated in lower skilled manufacturing jobs (Campbell et al. 1991, p. 180). Yet the backgrounds of immigrants from Vietnam were even more distant from unskilled manufacturing work than those of earlier arrivals. Further, they arrived at a time of job-shedding throughout Melbourne's manufacturing sector. This echoes findings from a study of migrant workers in Adelaide. Harrison (1984, p. 67) found immigrants disproportionately concentrated in manufacturing and construction, the very industry and occupational categories suffering the largest declines in employment in their study period of 1976-1982. Hence, the overwhelming importance of the manufacturing sector, especially for NESB immigrants, has been closely related neither to the prior employment experiences of migrants nor to the overall state of Australian manufacturing.

Clearly, segmentation of urban labour markets has shaped these experiences of immigrant workers. Segmentation is still not well understood at local scales (Peck 1996, pp. 87-96) but is underpinned by complex social and institutional processes which render the segments fluid and flexible rather than rigid and spatially invariant. At least four important processes have reinforced occupational and industrial segmentation of NESB migrants. First, some immigrants have faced restricted access to employment because of lower levels of skills relevant to the jobs available in metropolitan labour markets. Secondly, some have experienced significant non-recognition of overseas qualifications and smaller reward for education and training acquired overseas (Wooden 1994b, p. 249). Thirdly, there has been in some places a lack of opportunity for NESB migrants to reach proficiency in English which could open up employment prospects in a wider range of urban service industries. Finally, there has been a lack of opportunity for vocational training, especially workplace-based, especially in the industries with high concentrations of migrant workers. These processes are strongly gendered, producing quite different employment experiences for overseas-born women and men. Costs of urban housing, and the high propensities of migrants to become home-buyers, coupled with expenses of establishing households and family life, brought about higher participation rates among women from some NESB groups than among the Australian-born. Such women have been concentrated overwhelmingly in unskilled manufacturing jobs (Lack and Templeton 1995, p. 82), while other women have worked long hours as unwaged labour in family businesses.

All of these processes of segmentation work themselves out in particular places within the cities. Indeed, labour markets are constituted locally for all workers, not just migrants (Peck 1996, p. 95). Factors such as age, gender, ethnicity and a host of cultural considerations interact in particular places with questions of access to employment, distributions of local job opportunities, the distribution of housing opportunities, discrimination in both local housing and labour markets (see Hugo 1995, p. 18), local community resources and information networks. In the large cities, then, labour market outcomes for immigrants have been shaped powerfully by interactions between three things in the specific places where migrants have become concentrated.

1. Particular immigrant groups have become concentrated in inner city and outer suburban locations, partly because of historical availability of semi-skilled and unskilled jobs in these places, and also the availability of affordable housing to rent or purchase. The residential geography of initial settlers from particular groups is also important in helping to explain the geographical concentration of subsequent settlers from these groups. Yet by the 1990s, immigrants, and especially NESB groups, faced a restricted range of suitable employment opportunities in these parts of the city and often had poor access to jobs either in their local areas or in the wider metropolitan labour markets through commuting. Access to employment faced by any residential work force only partly reflects the location of jobs within the city and is shaped to a much greater extent by the different labour market experiences of these residents. In the case of NESB migrants, access has been affected strongly by their English language skills and by their qualifications.

2. Complex processes within households have shaped the participation rates and other labour market experiences of migrants, especially women. These include cultural factors, and female participation rates tend to be lowest within strongly patriarchal communities.

3. Access to employment is also shaped by social infrastructure, which is differently available in specific localities within the city. Among the most important have been affordable housing, child care and appropriate educational facilities. While housing availability has partly shaped the emergence of new outer suburban concentrations of NESB migrants in Sydney and Melbourne, these areas commonly experience

much lower per capita availability of important social infrastructure and this has further confined immigrants, both recent arrivals and NESB people more generally, into particular segments of the labour market which are often quite localised.

The employment experiences of the overseas-born throughout the 1980s and 1990s have been set in a context dominated by structural change and globalisation, which are really two sides of one coin (see Fagan and Webber 1994). Yet it is very important not to elevate these forces as sole determinants of the changed context. There have been major social and cultural changes too, including the profound impacts of the women's movement, which have affected the employment aspirations and labour market experiences of younger NESB women. Major increases in the participation of women in waged work and the rise of equal opportunity legislation have also been important. There have also been significant political changes, with governments seeking to balance budgets at Federal and State levels, often with cuts to expenditure on the social infrastructure which had supported growing suburban populations of the 1960s and 1970s.

The de-industrialisation of the Australian labour force since the early 1980s has particularly affected workers in Melbourne, Sydney and Adelaide. In these cities it has had a disproportionate impact on immigrants, both female and male. In Sydney, for example, impacts have varied considerably among different migrant groups. The proportionate loss of manufacturing jobs has been greatest among longer-established groups such as Italians, Greeks and people from the former Yugoslavia (Tait and Gibson 1987) and lowest among recently arrived groups such as the Vietnamese. The strong shift in the labour market of Australia's large cities towards services and jobs in the information economy has meant that traditional sites of migrant incorporation into waged work have diminished sharply. Hence, NESB migrants have faced a dramatic change in the availability, composition and nature of jobs. The rapid growth of the service sector has not produced jobs accessible to NESB migrant groups either locationally or in terms of their English proficiency and recognised qualifications.

Immigration and unemployment

De-industrialisation of Australia's metropolitan labour markets has been accompanied by the now well-known trends in unemployment. Figure 7.2 shows the varied experiences of the largest Australian State capital cities. Yet these aggregate trends disguise more than they reveal since the incidence of high unemployment rates is localised within the cities. Figure 7.3 shows rates for a selection of SLAs in Sydney. While SLAs do not define local labour markets, the graph illustrates strong local variation in the experiences of unemployment within Australia's largest city and principal target for overseas migrants since 1980. Middle class suburbs to the north and south of Sydney exhibit rates of unemployment well below national averages (some not much above those of the long boom). By sharp contrast, inner and outer suburban SLAs contain some of Australia's highest rates of unemployment. In the early 1980s the working-class inner city SLA of Marrickville, with a high proportion of NESB migrants among its residents, showed unemployment rates among the highest in the metropolitan area. Yet by 1993, its rate had fallen to no more than the Sydney average, reflecting some out-migration of established immigrant groups to the suburbs but, in particular, continued gentrification of the SLA through in-migration of information workers.

By 1993, the highest rates of unemployment in Sydney were found in the outer western and south-western suburbs. These labour market dislocations reflect complex causal processes and are no simple reflection of any one factor, least of all levels of immigration. The youthful nature of the labour force in outer suburban SLAs clearly underpins the future growth-rate of demand for jobs well into the next century. Suburbanisation has caused the location of Sydney's resident labour force, especially its industrial labour force, to move westward steadily since the early 1960s. Yet in the recent past, this growth of population and higher rates of household formation have stimulated new employment in the suburbs, for example in building and construction, small-scale manufacturing and retailing. They do not, in themselves, explain the puzzle of Western Sydney's high jobless rates in the 1990s, certainly not among its NESB groups.

Most published economic analysis, conducted largely at the national aggregate scale, has on the whole dismissed claims that immigration and these levels of unemployment can be related directly. According to an influential study by Withers and Pope (1985, p. 560), 'immigration policy need not be dominated by fear of immigration causing unemployment'. Yet these conclusions were based on their findings that, since the beginning of post-War immigration, 'migrants have created at least as many jobs as they have occupied' (1985, p. 562). While there is little recent evidence to contradict their findings overall, the rates of unemployment among some immigrant groups in specific parts of Australia's largest cities have been alarming since the early 1980s. Further, the mean duration of unemployment in April 1994 for NESB immigrants was 74 weeks, compared to 54.8 weeks for migrants from English-speaking countries, and 52 weeks for Australian-born (Murphy and Watson 1994).

Figure 7.2 Unemployment 1984-1993, Australian Capital Cities

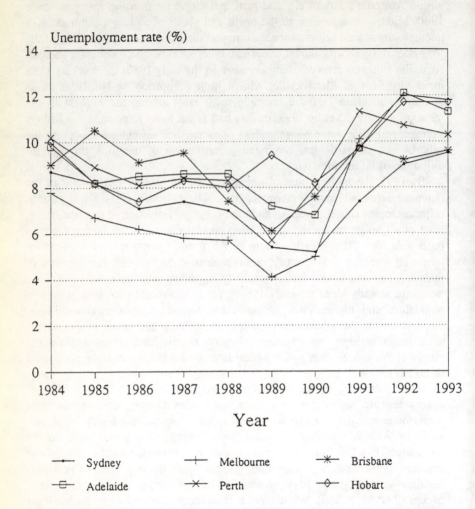

Source: Commonwealth of Australia, Department of Employment, Education and Training (1984-1993) Statistics (various years)

Figure 7.2 Unemployment 1984-1993, selected Sydney Statistical Local Areas

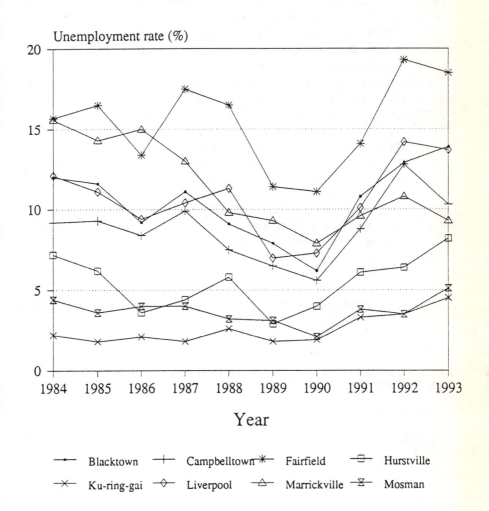

Source: Commonwealth of Australia, Department of Employment, Education and Training (1984-1993) Statistics (various years)

Rates of joblessness have differed markedly among various immigrant groups (Table 7.2). At the 1991 census, they were highest among people from Lebanon (25 per cent compared with rates among the Australian-born of 10 per cent) and Vietnam (24.5 per cent). There is not a simple dichotomy between English-speaking and NESB migrants. Unemployment rates were lowest in 1991 among migrants from Italy (6.3 per cent), United Kingdom (6.5 per cent) and Greece (7.9 per cent) – all lower rates than those among the Australian-born. Experiences of women and men differed quite strongly with female rates lower than those for males in some groups but higher in others. Participation rates are crucial here. While unemployment rates for Lebanese women were very much lower than those for Lebanese men (Table 7.2), their participation rate was only 32 per cent compared with the rate for Australian-born females of 57 per cent. Time of arrival and migration status are important in explaining these overall differences between NESB groups over the last ten years. A high proportion of Vietnamese and Lebanese immigrants are recent arrivals with mostly refugee or family reunion status. McAllister (1991) shows that for the Lebanese and Vietnamese, two birthplace groups with the highest proportions of recently-arrived migrants, levels of unemployment have fluctuated between 20 and 30 per cent since 1980.

Table 7.2 Unemployment rates by birthplace and gender, Australia 1991 (per cent in work force)

	Male	Female	Total
Australian-born	8.0	6.9	7.5
Overseas-born	10.2	9.4	9.9
UK/Eire	7.6	5.0	6.5
Italy	6.1	6.6	6.3
Greece	6.9	9.7	7.9
Former Yugoslavia	10.6	12.1	11.2
Lebanon	30.8	12.3	25.1
Vietnam	24.5	30.5	26.8

Source: Australian Bureau of Statistics (1991b)

By 1993, some of the highest rates of unemployment in Sydney's vulnerable outer western suburbs were being experienced by NESB groups (females and males). The most severe localised unemployment was found in suburbs with high concentrations of recently-arrived migrants, such as Fairfield and Liverpool – both, ironically, SLAs which experienced rapid growth of new jobs between 1985 and 1993. Problems of access to employment for new settlers in these SLAs are reinforced by lack of English proficiency, even when people can speak several other languages, especially in localities where accessible manufacturing jobs are disappearing through de-industrialisation. By 1995, there were still high rates of participation in manufacturing by both male and female NESB workers throughout Sydney. Jobs in the service sector often remained inaccessible, although they were often located in the same or adjacent SLAs, especially to retrenched manufacturing workers and young people from NESB groups.

Hence, the limited research findings specifically dealing with recent experiences in the large cities show that rates of unemployment among immigrants depend most significantly on their birthplace and, for NESB immigrants, their English-language proficiency and length of residence (Wooden 1994b, p. 231). Inglis and Stromback (1986) argue that for migrants as a whole, length of residence has been of greatest importance. The chances of newly-arrived migrants joining the ranks of the unemployed are influenced strongly by the overall state of the labour market at their time of arrival, especially locally in the inner city and suburban locations which still receive most NESB migrants. Burnley's study of recently-arrived Vietnamese migrants found that 'it is not absolutely clear whether discrimination in the labour market has been a significant factor in high unemployment' (Burnley 1989, p. 149). Rather, research suggests that proficiency in English universally remains a crucial factor in determining an immigrant's chances of obtaining a job.

Female job-seekers in the outer suburbs are often discouraged if employment appropriate to their qualifications, available working hours, and daily domestic responsibilities such as child care, are not available locally or accessible by their various transport options. For most outer suburban women, access to a motor vehicle has become a key to daily mobility including the journey to work (Croft 1996). This access is lower for women in some NESB groups than among the Australian-born. In addition, lack of affordable child care facilities reduces dramatically the job-opportunities of primary care-givers (by 1995 still mostly women) especially in single-parent families. These problems are faced by outer suburban women whether they are immigrants or Australian-born. For a large number of outer suburban women, not simply those from NESB groups, entry to waged work in the 1990s has come through casual jobs with no security of tenure and low wages (Fagan 1995).

Diffusion of English language skills is a highly gendered process depending on contact patterns often geared to workplaces. Married women from strongly patriarchal cultural groups often gain least exposure to English language. Jamrozik (1991) also shows that among NESB immigrants, educational and occupational qualifications on arrival are not related significantly to employment chances. Such skills often remain poorly utilised within the urban economies because of segmentation in their local labour markets and the processes by which NESB migrants enter employment. Finally, research shows that the tendency towards above-average unemployment rates falls as the period of residence increases. Significantly, however, NESB women in general and males from Middle Eastern and Asian countries have not shown this decline over time in rates of unemployment. Hence, it is not surprising that migrant women in outer suburbs face highly restricted entry points to waged-work opportunities, showing a disproportionate representation in secondary labour market practices such as sweatshops and outworking. In 1996, a Senate inquiry heard evidence that outworkers in Sydney and Melbourne from NESB groups are among the lowest paid workers in Australia.

Immigration and labour markets in the cities:
a summary

The evidence reviewed in this chapter suggests that, far from taking the jobs of Australian residents since the early 1980s, recently-arrived immigrants from non English-speaking backgrounds have experienced high initial unemployment rates because they are unable to wrest their share of jobs away from residents already entrenched in the labour market (Harrison 1984). Labour market experiences of both overseas-born groups and the Australian-born are strongly shaped by factors at the local level interacting with national and global economic change, changes in the social and political regulation of labour markets, and significant shifts in government policy aimed at reducing budget deficits. Outer suburban areas of Sydney and Melbourne are not intrinsically regions where high unemployment has been concentrated historically, any more than their residents can be described as necessarily socially disadvantaged or different to other suburban populations. During the 1960s, when suburbanisation first accelerated, these areas shared the national condition of near full employment, although it must be remembered that participation rates for women were much lower and female unemployment rates were twice those for men throughout the 1960s. In the 1990s, significant groups of outer suburban residents have been marginalised by the economic and political changes. There is no doubt that NESB migrants, especially those from recently-arrived groups, make up a disproportionate share of these marginalised people in the largest capital cities.

Further moves to deregulate labour markets, to the extent that they contribute to growth of secondary labour markets in the cities, could disadvantage these groups even more. Rather than taking jobs from Australian-born residents, immigrants seem to have borne a disproportionate share of the impact of economic and political restructuring on the cities while continuing to add their weight as consumers to the growth in demand for goods and services. Although much greater research is needed, the evidence assembled to date suggests that longer-established immigrants, even from the most vulnerable communities, have improving employment experiences over time, are recognised widely in the literature as hard-working and highly-motivated (although it is easy to simply rely on caricatures here) and show higher rates of self-employment than the Australian-born.

Hence, unemployment in Australian cities has been one of the uneven local outcomes of globalisation and de-industrialisation, and NESB migrants have been strongly affected. It is important to note that by 1996, unemployment rates in outer suburban Sydney remained well above national averages. These higher rates were most noticeable among people in the 15 to 24 years age-group (both Australian-born and overseas-born) and among Australian-born males over 50 years old. Clearly, outer suburban unemployment cannot be identified simplistically with the concentration of particular groups of NESB migrants. All groups have been affected by restructuring. Governments have implemented strategies purposefully to facilitate and encourage this restructuring and to 'internationalise' the Australian economy either in the knowledge that the impacts will be socially uneven, commonly arguing the impacts to be temporary problems of adjustment to necessary change, or misunderstanding the importance of local processes in determining who wins and loses from restructuring. Because of this, recent arguments that immigration should be curtailed because of high rates of urban unemployment are simplistic. At worst, they verge on blaming immigrants (usually those from NESB groups) for their own labour market problems.

Such arguments also take attention away from the complex combinations of global, national and local forces which cause unemployment in the work force at large. Solutions to unemployment in the cities will require not just further job-creation through economic growth but serious attempts by Federal and State governments to come to grips with social infrastructure deficiencies in the rapidly-growing outer suburbs. If the Australian government's immigration policies are to contribute to the search for solutions to unemployment, then they could be coordinated with industry policy (e.g. in planning the skill-composition of the annual intake) and constructed with greater regional and local sensitivity.

Yet because of the difficulties in connecting immigration intake to economic issues, immigration policy should be decided on grounds other than stereotypes about the assumed difficulties faced in urban labour markets by people of non English-speaking background.

chapter eight

Regional development

In a July 1996 media release, headlined 'Migrants Encouraged to Settle Away from Major Cities', the Minister for Immigration and Multicultural Affairs, Mr Philip Ruddock, said:

> in response to community input, the Government is developing a series of measures which will stimulate the social and economic development of the less populous states and regions of Australia.

This move reflects quite disparate political positions regarding the settlement pattern of recent immigrants across the set of Australian cities and regions. On the one hand, politicians from Victoria and New South Wales argue that their capital cities receive too many immigrants. These 'immigrant surplus' States perceive that, while they may indeed be receiving benefits from immigration, they are being asked to carry a disproportionate share of the public sector and social costs associated with population growth and household formation. It was pointed out in earlier chapters that the present government of New South Wales represents this position most strongly. Such political stances are inextricably bound up with long-running debates about regional economic development in Australia, including the diseconomies of size associated with the larger cities that have been addressed in the body of this book.

On the other hand, there are those States and territories whose governments perceive that they are not obtaining a fair share of the benefits which immigrants are presumed to bring with them to regional economies. South Australia, Tasmania and the Northern Territory are most notable here (Dawkins 1991; Perron 1993). These 'immigrant deficit' regions perceive that immigrants will assist their populations to grow and that this will lead to economic growth as immigrants set up businesses, provide skills in short supply, and create demand for local goods and services. Queensland and Western Australia stand in a more or less neutral position inasmuch as their economies are relatively buoyant but their capitals are small enough to have not yet accumulated the diseconomies of urban size that are so pronounced in Sydney and Melbourne. In any case, those States already attract significant shares of immigrants to Australia.

These polarised stances, and the response of the Australian government to them as part of the politics of federalism – well illustrated by the above quote from the Minister for Immigration – rest on contestable assumptions. Those who argue that cities like Sydney receive too many immigrants base their case on the issues discussed in earlier chapters. To recapitulate, critics say that environmental pressures resulting from population growth are unsustainable, demands for urban infrastructure cannot be met, or at least cannot be met in socially acceptable ways, and that access to affordable housing in large cities is disproportionately low compared with the smaller cities. The States whose governments wish to attract more immigrants base their arguments on presumed skill shortages and on the view that by increasing their populations they will be better able to build economies which can compete with the likes of Sydney and Melbourne.

Issues in Australian regional development

In order to evaluate these claims – and by extension to evaluate the prospects for influencing the location decisions of immigrants – some of the context of the history of Australian regional development processes and policy is needed. Two aspects of Australia's system of cities and regions have long driven the rhetoric and practice of regional development planning. First, there is the set of problems arising from the fact that most of the State capital cities are very much larger than the next largest urban centres in their respective States. Secondly, there is the fact that New South Wales and Victoria have always dominated the Australian economy while the other States have been relegated to an economically peripheral role and have depended on tax transfers from the south-eastern States to fund their public sector spending commitments. Each of these matters will now be considered in a little detail.

Metropolitan primacy

The dominance of most of the capital cities in their States has been referred to as a condition of 'metropolitan primacy'. Sydney, for example, contains just over 60 per cent of New South Wales's population, Melbourne 70 per cent of Victoria's and Perth 72 per cent of Western Australia's. This means that there have been relatively few business and employment opportunities generated in medium sized and smaller cities. The capitals, especially Sydney and Melbourne, have thus become what many would regard as oversized.

But what is meant by oversized? In order to properly debate this notion a little urban economic theory is required. Specifically, the concepts of agglomeration economies and diseconomies need to be considered. These notions parallel, and to all intents and purposes incorporate, the notion of externalities which was deployed in Chapter 6 as part of the examination of the relationship between population size and urban environmental quality. Agglomeration economies are simply those benefits which businesses and people obtain from living in a larger city but which they do not have to pay to create. Businesses benefit from, among other things: greater access to specialised business services and sub-contractors; the availability of larger pools of variably skilled labour; superior training facilities; and opportunities to specialise in larger and more diversified markets for goods and services. People benefit from, for example, the availability of more specialised goods and services and a wider range of jobs.

An interesting sidelight on the immigration question is the way in which multiculturalism has been used to actively market Australian cities to businesses and tourists. A striking feature of the final issue of 'Share the Spirit', one of the Sydney Olympic Bid Committee's products, is its focus on Sydney's multicultural character: 'Sydney says "welcome!" in many languages'. Two pages are devoted to ethnic Australia, including a whole page showing numbers of people by birthplace. Multiculturalism is deployed as a marketing strategy. As an Australian immigration officer based in Hong Kong said: 'We push the line of multiculturalism at a million miles an hour'.

Generally speaking, at least up to a point, agglomeration economies increase as a city's population grows. Since agglomeration economies attract both business investment and people, economic and population growth becomes self-perpetuating; agglomeration economies beget growth and growth augments the level of agglomeration economies. The other side to the growth coin is diseconomies of agglomeration, such as higher levels of road congestion and air pollution. In principle, an optimal size for a city may be imagined as the size at which agglomeration economies and diseconomies balance out. At this point, if some simplifying assumptions are made, a city should stop growing and any growth impetus in the national economy should be displaced to cities which have not yet achieved an optimum size. Chief among the simplifying assumptions required to make this a reasonable inference is that agglomeration economies and diseconomies are equally shared across a city's population. This is patently not the case because a higher income will enable greater access to agglomeration economies, such as high-quality entertainment, while simultaneously facilitating avoidance of diseconomies, such as traffic congestion.

The problem of city size was first addressed in the *Sydney Region Outline Plan* of 1968 (NSW State Planning Authority 1968). Due to immigration-driven population growth in the 1950s and 1960s, combined with an explosion of automobile ownership which was a key factor in massive suburban housing development, a view had been formed by many that the city was growing too large. As a result:

> the State Planning Authority . . . concluded that an integral part of the population strategy for the Sydney Region should be the adoption of a provisional aim to steer 500,000 of Sydney's projected growth to new centres in other areas of the State. (p. 19)

This statement illustrates the type of thinking which underpinned the joint Commonwealth–State growth centres program of the 1970s that focussed on Bathurst-Orange in New South Wales and Albury-Wodonga on the border of New South Wales and Victorian. It was thought that by stimulating economic growth in a small number of carefully selected non-metropolitan urban centres that agglomeration economies would accumulate to a point where growth would be self-perpetuating and the centres would then become counterweights to the large metropolitan cities.

The economics of city size was a very active area of research in the 1960s and early 1970s and the doyen of urban and regional economics, H. Richardson, comprehensively reviewed this material in a book published in 1973. He concluded that many of the economies and diseconomies of urban size were unmeasurable or that, where they were measurable, were incommensurate with each other. He concluded that any focus on urban size as a variable to be manipulated by public policy was thus misguided.

More recently Tolley and Crihfield (1987) outlined the conventional wisdom regarding attempts to deal with urban problems by manipulating the location of population and economic activity. Their surmisal echoes the analysis presented in Chapter 6 in relation to urban environmental issues:

> A first best solution, to be strongly recommended, is to adopt policies that directly internalise the externalities. If externalities are internalised there would be no departure of actual from optimal city sizes and hence no need for city size or other locational policies. In a second best world, where externalities are not completely internalised, a case can be made in principle for indirectly attacking externalities by trying to influence the location of activities. If uninternalised externalities are greater in one place than another, there is a potential net gain from fostering a shift in location. In contrast to direct locational incentives, more promising could be to help improve government resource allocation decisions . . . especially vis-a-vis decisions with direct locational effects, such as roads, transit, water resources.

As Einstein is reputed to have said, there is nothing more practical than a good theory. On a less theoretical tack though, and taking an historical perspective, the early 1970s saw the onset of what appeared to be a sea change in the dominance of large cities. Demographic data from all parts of the western industrialised world began to show, in the early 1970s, that many large cities were losing their shares of national population with the slack being taken up by non-metropolitan urban centres and rural areas. Sydney's share of New South Wales's population declined, for example, from 63.8 per cent in 1971 to 61.7 per cent in 1991; the figures for Melbourne were 71.9 per cent and 70.9 per cent respectively. This trend came to be known as 'counter-urbanisation' or – more accurately, since most of the non-metropolitan growth was in small urban centres rather than spread across the countryside – the 'population turnaround'. This trend held out the prospect that the day of the mega-city had ended. A reasonable inference was that policy to curtail metropolitan growth was now redundant because market forces were accomplishing planning objectives as people and businesses voted with their feet against large cities. The population turnaround has continued but in a more muted form in recent years. Moreover, while in Australia the turnaround held out some prospects for growth in non-metropolitan areas, especially on the coast, the trend has not been unambiguously beneficial. Coastal amenity regions – such as the north coast of New South Wales and south-east Queensland – which have been the beneficiaries of growth also typically experience very high unemployment rates. Moreover, whatever job and business growth as there has been in such regions is typically narrowly-based in tourism and retirement migration with little evidence of the emergence of dynamic, diversified economies. With this sort of competition the day of the large city is hardly over. Indeed, far from being redundant, the large city is arguably even more strongly entrenched as the locus of late 20th century economic growth.

More significant than non-metropolitan population growth within the Australian States, from the point of view of the issues concerning politicians in cities like Sydney and Melbourne, has been the growth of cities like Perth and Brisbane. These places now arguably embody agglomeration economies at levels that will strongly encourage, if not guarantee, their future growth. They may therefore be increasingly considered as serious alternatives to Sydney and Melbourne as places to live and do business. The growth of Perth and Brisbane can to some significant degree be interpreted as the outcome of people voting with their feet against the larger, older cities of the south-east.

Competitive advantage of regions

As noted above, the second major feature of Australia's economic geography which has driven regional development policy has been the economic domination of New South Wales and Victoria, specifically their respective capital cities of Sydney and Melbourne, in the national system of cities and regions. This imbalance has been redressed to some extent since the early 1970s by growth in the sunbelt States of Queensland and Western Australia, based especially on tourism and minerals exports. Against this, New South Wales and Victoria have suffered most from the loss of manufacturing jobs since the early 1970s.

Illustrating the implications of these shifts for immigrant location choices, a recent ministerial press release trumpeted:

> Business Migration gives major boost to the Qld economy.
>
> Queensland has been one of the most successful states in attracting investment linked migration; nearly half the Australian investment total of 140 million. Some 20 per cent of all business migrants including those in the investment linked category, settle in Queensland. (media release, 26 November 1996, Minister for Immigration and Multicultural Affairs)

Melbourne, and especially Sydney, still however capture a large share of national economic growth. The extent to which immigration directly and indirectly influences, or may be made to influence – through public policy – these imbalances in the national settlement system, has been of considerable interest to State and Australian governments in recent years.

Policy options: general

There is an argument that immigrants might be encouraged to settle in what are now deficit regions. Two possibilities are to manipulate the points system – used by the Australian government to select immigrants – and to improve the information which is made available to immigrants prior to their making decisions to migrate to Australia.

The problem with manipulating the points system is that location weights, in order to have a discernible effect, may have to be so high that they would dominate in the selection process. The overall 'quality' – in terms of skills, health status, English language capability and so forth – of immigrants may thus be lowered and this would have negative implications for the national economy. A second problem, in principle, with using the points system is that once people have settled in a deficit region, it is impossible, under current laws and customs, to compel them to stay there for any length of time. If there were higher personal returns to be obtained by moving to other parts of Australia then immigrants would eventually relocate themselves.

It is possible that if immigrants were somehow encouraged to settle in deficit regions then they might discover advantages existing there and stay on in perpetuity. Perceptual knowledge of these destinations might thus build up among potential immigrants and they would then be increasingly favoured in location decisions. This seems a reasonable argument since perceptual knowledge is one of the fundamental determinants of regional economic growth: people minimise the potential costs of settlement decisions by colonising known, large places since information is expensive to accumulate. Tinkering with 'official' information supplied to people considering migration to Australia is however unlikely to have more than a marginal effect on choices since people are already required to be quite well-informed before serious consideration is given to applications to migrate. In any case, much of the knowledge used by immigrants comes from prior immigrants and from experience, such as that accumulated through visits for education, business or recreational tourism. Such perceptual knowledge comes from experience rather than from the written texts which might be supplied by government authorities seeking to attract investment to cities and regions.

Recent policy initiatives

In spite of these cautionary words, the Australian Government proposed a number of initiatives in 1996 to address some of the concerns of both 'surplus' and 'deficit' regions. These are now outlined.

Regional Sponsored Migration Scheme

The Regional Sponsored Migration Scheme is aimed at assisting the economic development of regional and low-growth areas of Australia. Broadly, the scheme enables employers in these areas, who are unable to meet their skilled work-force needs from the local labour market, to nominate people from overseas or already in Australia temporarily, to settle and work in their region.

The scheme is designed to complement special migration arrangements already in place to encourage migrants to settle in low growth areas of Australia. These include:

- awarding an additional 5 points under the Concessional Family category to migration applicants whose sponsors live in a designated low-growth area; and
- setting aside up to 15 places each year for each State and Territory to sponsor business migrants who would benefit the development of their State or Territory but who would not meet selection requirements without bonus points for sponsorship.

Proposed bond scheme

On 5 July 1996 the Australian Government floated a 'bond scheme' as part of a package of policy measures designed to address the imbalance in the migration program, thus explicitly accepting the viewpoint that too many immigrants settle in Sydney and Melbourne. One measure, designed to have immediate effect, was to involve the setting aside of 700 concessional places for migrants sponsored by relatives in regional and rural areas. The government was also looking at redirecting skilled migrants to less populated regions, allowing people who just fall short of eligibility requirements to take up work in designated regions. To ensure that such immigrants stay in the regions, the Federal government proposed a bond system. Immigrants would be required to post bonds of up to $30,000 before arrival and would forfeit the money if they subsequently moved to more populated areas.

In spite of these policy initiatives, the fact remains that for immigrant deficit regions, at least up until recent years, other than through 'chain migration' (whereby people settle in places to which friends and relatives have previously migrated), the fact that immigrants are not choosing such regions in significant numbers is in fact an indicator of their relatively lower growth prospects (Lewis 1992). Immigrants are not settling in large numbers in such regions because they perceive their prospects as being better elsewhere.

In politicised language, the Minister for Immigration responded to criticisms of these initiatives by suggesting, in a media release of 10 July 1996, that 'Critics Miss Point on Migrant Dispersal'. He said:

> Opponents would have you believe that the only cities anyone should settle in, are Sydney or Melbourne. Both are magnificent cities, but we should be encouraging migrants to also consider other parts of Australia. Cities such as Adelaide, Darwin, Hobart and Cairns are saying they have specific skills shortages they cannot fill locally. The schemes outlined or being considered by the Government will help meet those needs by bringing in highly skilled migrants. It is wrong of people to say there are no opportunities in those cities.

The same media release went on to suggest:

> Some people are tilting at windmills in their criticism [of the 700 migrants plan]. The facts are:
>
> - there is no proposal to place a large number of unskilled migrants into areas without job prospects. The people entering will be highly skilled;
>
> - there is no coercion. People who wish to settle in the major population centres can still apply under the remaining 72,800 places in other categories;
>
> - the possible performance bond has been blown out of proportion. The new category does not have a bond and will rely on the attraction of the family sponsor.

The Minister claimed that the Regional Sponsored Migration Scheme (RSMS) had already filled a skill vacuum for employers in Tasmania, the Northern Territory and Western Australia.

In an attempt to further bolster support for his initiatives, the Minister made another media release on 10 July 1996, claiming that his 'Migrant settlement proposals offer freedom of choice.' He said that:

138

- If a bond were to be implemented, migrants would still be free to move and decide where they want to live in Australia, but there would be consequences of breaking their promise. I don't regard this as an unreasonable restriction in relation to movement.

- Those who oppose or try to dismiss the ideas are ignoring the wishes of the community and will undermine public confidence in the migration program.

- The misinformed debate on these measures is disappointing. The 1200 places identified specifically for migration away from major population centres account for less than two per cent of the overall Program. Any further developments will be of the same order of magnitude.

Ironically, the task force set up to consider the use of financial penalties to force migrants to settle away from the major population centres subsequently acknowledged that the scheme would be too difficult to enforce. In a *Sydney Morning Herald* article of 13 March 1997, headed 'Migrant bond plan put in the too hard basket', Michael Millett reported that the idea was to be formally scrapped at a meeting of Commonwealth and State ministers the next day. Millett said:

> The task force report . . . is understood to argue that migrant settlement patterns are best addressed by a concerted government approach, particularly through regional development policies which deal with wider population movements. It argues that migrants will continue to settle where there are family links or where job opportunities are greatest and that measures to force them to live elsewhere will be ineffective and impossible to police.

This much could readily have been concluded before the task force commenced its work.

Conclusion

The idea that growth pressures in the larger Australian cities may be alleviated, and that regional development in the States with less buoyant economies may be enhanced by the policy-driven steering of immigrants to preferred parts of Australia is flawed in theory and in practice. Current attempts by the Australian Government in this regard owe more to ministerial perceptions of the politics of the immigration program than to the realities of controlling the location of population and economic activity. In truth the only policy initiatives which will influence location patterns are those which address the sources of negative externalities in urban settings. The strongest evidence for this is in the net internal migration losses experienced by Sydney and Melbourne for the past quarter century (Murphy 1993). People are literally voting with their feet and effective policy to 'internalise externalities' will accentuate changes in behaviour which are needed to deal with city growth pressures. Combined with the emergence of competitive advantages in, particularly, Queensland and Western Australia, migration from the south-eastern States will continue to be a significant part of the process of adaptation to adverse living and working conditions in the largest cities. In fact this brief primer on the realities of economic development processes and policy options is probably understood by government since the minister's proposals are so modest. They may be worth experimenting with and probably assist in the politics of Federal–State relationships but they will do next to nothing either to promote regional development or to deal with growth pressures in the largest cities. It really gets back to the issues raised in Chapter 6. That is, the conflicting agendas of supporters of immigration, environmentalists and those concerned with social justice. Admittedly finding a way through that political minefield is not easy, and perhaps honest if marginal efforts should be applauded.

chapter nine

Conclusion

We have described the recent growth in Australia's metropolitan cities and, from several points of view, the role of immigration in growth has been examined. This book is thus a response to the at times intense public debate over the positive and negative impact of immigrants on Australia's society, economy, and environment. In brief, several commentators have argued that immigration has exacerbated urban problems, and in particular metropolitan problems. Before this assertion is renewed, it may fairly be stated that key urban problems are societal problems rather than problems of cities per se. Even the cost of infrastructure may be seen as a societal problem, in terms of taxation levels and sources, revenue allocation, the willingness of people to pay, the ability of managerial elites to adequately forecast demand, and problems arising from overseas borrowing for improvements. The issue of whether there are ghettos may also be seen as a societal problem, because of the nature of segregative processes, as well as the related issue of who is segregating themselves from whom. Are ghettos social constructions of the dominant society (assuming that they exist)?

Immigration as a problem for cities

Immigration has been singled out by many commentators as a problem for the cities because of concerns about overall rates of population growth, infrastructure provision, road congestion, declining urban amenity, housing costs and pollution. This is partly because Australia does not have a comprehensive population policy. It is also because, in a situation of population fertility levels being below the level required to achieve zero population growth, immigration naturally becomes a significant component of population growth. It is, however, doubtful whether Australia needs a population policy other than common sense about what is a reasonable level of immigration and growth, given environmental and economic constraints and opportunities which exist in Australia. Certainly, the notion of determination of an optimum population is not taken seriously by most social scientists and an increasing number of natural scientists are sceptical about the value of this concept and its quantification. Nevertheless a few well-respected natural scientists argue for an ultimate human population of 10 million in Australia (compared with the 1997 estimate of 18.35 million) as desirable from a local environmental point of view and in terms of global environmental responsibilities. At this point the issues become complex because of the relative value being placed on the environment and on human welfare more generally.

However, relatively few immigrants, especially those of non English-speaking background, settle outside the capital cities and the secondary industrial cities of Newcastle and Wollongong. Immigration has been relatively slight in the other secondary industrial cities of Whyalla in South Australia, and Geelong and the Latrobe Valley complex in Victoria in recent years. Indeed the share of immigration to Adelaide and Hobart has diminished in the last 20 years so that there are now four principal foci for immigration: Sydney, Melbourne, Perth and Canberra. While immigration to Brisbane is of significance, it is less than internal migration from elsewhere in Australia to that city. Immigration in itself does not result in an increasing spread of population around the nation: it is internal migration that is giving rise to urbanisation pressures along the non-metropolitan sections of the coastal strip of eastern Australia. Of course the cities as focal points of population growth and consumption make increasing impacts on the ecumene and the natural environment. It is our view, however, that it is the nature of the urban lifestyle and economic system, which creates the negative economic impacts, that is the issue rather than population growth. Secondly, it is the adequacy of urban management – and its associated politics – that is the issue rather than population growth. If, though, there are more households, then the demand for services and consumption will increase, unless individual households moderate their demands for services and their consumption.

Immigration and other factors
in the demand for housing

Discussion of households raises the issue of the impact of both household growth, and the characteristics of households, on the demand for housing and urban residential expansion. We have examined the role of the components of growth in population in Australia in the recent past and have established that, despite the lower level of population fertility in Australia, natural increase is still significant, although its rate is slowly declining. Associated with this natural increase is a relatively high rate of household formation that is critical in the demand for housing associated with the lateral spread of suburbia. Household growth rates have been 75 to 100 per cent above the rates of total population growth in several of the mainland metropolitan cities. These high rates of household growth result from several demographic factors of which current immigration is only one. These factors include the size of the age cohorts in the family-forming and 'coupling' age range; current immigration; the impact of higher birth rates in the past quarter century; lapses between these births and their forming new households as adults; and the impact of higher levels of immigration in the past. In the late 1950s, 1960s and early 1970s immigration was strongly concentrated in the 18 to 30 years age range and 80 per cent of migrants commenced their family formation in Australia. The result has been that, a generation hence, the children of these families have matured and created new families. Changes in marriage rates also affect new household formation and therefore the demand for housing, especially with the high rates of marital dissolution and remarriage. Another influence is the increased longevity of the population, as a result of what has been termed the 'second demographic transition'. Mortality has declined considerably in Australia and other developed countries since the mid-1960s, particularly at ages over 35. Life expectancy has increased by more than eight years in that time. This means that there are many more older people occupying housing that, a generation earlier, would have been occupied by younger families (sometimes their offspring via inheritance) through the demise of the older people. The problem from an urban planning perspective is that the quantitative (and therefore relative) importance of all these (and other) variables on household formation have not been analytically determined at the national, State or metropolitan level in Australia. Furthermore, their relative importance is likely to change over time, and to vary considerably at the local level.

Immigration and urban infrastructure

In considering the resource costs of supplying urban infrastructure and the recovery of costs for services, one problem is the low density and sprawling nature of our cities. A central facet of the Australia lifestyle as it has evolved has been the detached suburban house on its own block of land. This desire for space, both historically and at an accentuated pace during the period of the long post-war economic boom, was reinforced by the authoritative notion that the successful (man) was one who could afford an owner-occupied and separate house on its own suburban block. Living at medium density, despite the long-term social and economic success of medium and even higher density, 4 to 7 storey apartment housing in most sizeable continental European cities, it was not (and some say still is not) seen as fully socially acceptable. There was thus much negative stereotyping of medium-density and high-rise housing. This meant that large-scale, low-density suburbanisation was inevitable in the Australian context. Such low densities meant that public transport was an uneconomic proposition and would run at a loss as far as the middle ring and outer suburban components of the public transport networks in the metropolitan cities were concerned. Affluence and the motor car, of course, made low-density suburbanisation even more feasible. Ultimately, gentrification meant the re-appraisal of higher-density terrace housing environments in the inner city and the cost of housing there rose (particularly in Sydney) relative to that at the metropolitan periphery. Resulting price pressures pushed outer suburbanisation, at low densities, even further afield.

The key items of infrastructure which have to be funded include public transport, electricity, gas reticulation, telephone reticulation (which with partial privatisation now yields profits), sewerage reticulation, water reticulation, roading, kerbing, schools, hospitals and the maintenance of all these. A more recent trend has been that development companies pay at least some of the infrastructure costs associated with developments. Of course, as far as residential developments are concerned, it is generally accepted that these developer costs are passed on to the consumer, that is, the purchaser of the house and land packages. The cost to the public purse is however considerable in the case of new residential subdivisions per housing allotment. Immigrants, though, do not normally settle directly in new residential subdivisions on the periphery, so it is other demographic processes that are dominant in the demand for new housing on the periphery.

Immigration and urban consolidation

One response to these pressures is urban consolidation, that is, increasing residential densities in established areas, and new housing areas on the edge of the city, mostly in the latter case via villa units, smaller housing lots, dual occupancies or walk-up apartments. Urban consolidation is strongly favoured by many politicians and a number of planners on the basis that it will reduce transport congestion via the motor car, make the local use of infrastructure more economic and slow the outward spread of the cities. Other planners note that most medium-density developments in Sydney have been taking place in outer fringe localities, with only 10 per cent being built in established suburbs. In addition, the dual occupancy component of urban consolidation has proved unpopular in a number of localities because it contributes to more parking in streets and greater traffic densities in streets not designed for them. Furthermore, there is considerable evidence that the redevelopments at higher residential densities in the inner and middle ring areas of cities, whether in residential neighbourhoods or on vacated industrial and government land, are primarily middle-income or higher-income developments. Hence they cannot in reality house significant numbers of low-income families who would otherwise settle in low-cost housing estates on the metropolitan periphery. For these and other technical reasons associated with surveying and the engineering required for reticulation, urban consolidation will probably not slow significantly the outward march of suburbia (Troy 1996).

In any case, can it be argued that immigration has made urban consolidation necessary in the large cities? Certainly, past immigration has contributed significantly to the growth of metropolitan Sydney and Melbourne – now respectively at 3.8 and 3.5 million people – and their spatial spread because of the demand for housing. It should, though, be recalled that throughout the last 50 years immigration has played a strong replacement role in the established areas of cities where most immigrants have settled; the pre-existing population having partially moved to outer suburbs, having died or, in the case of Sydney and Melbourne, having migrated interstate or to the eastern coastal zone of Australia. The relatively modest immigration intake to Australia throughout the 1990s has not, however, created the need for urban consolidation (assuming that this need actually exists). If, though, Sydney becomes increasingly the focus of immigration, and if immigration returns to a higher level, it could be argued that immigration may contribute to the need for urban consolidation. On the other hand, immigrants have shown a tolerance for medium densities in the past, at least in the short term until they become economically established. Their residential preferences are soon, though, overwhelmingly those of mainstream Australians; that is, for relatively low density housing and surrounds. Furthermore, while some immigrants may show a tolerance for medium-density housing in the short term, there is no evidence as indicated by detailed census data, that there is significant crowding in accommodation, even with current recent arrivals. Immigrants do not cause crowding and higher densities. It is true, however, that there is considerable foreign ownership of high-density housing in Sydney's central business district, on its harbour foreshores and in its eastern suburbs (high-density housing being defined as that of four or more storeys). Much of this foreign ownership is by investors from Hong Kong, Singapore, Malaysia, North America and New Zealand. Furthermore, growing numbers of affluent locals are buying such housing to live in. Some of the overseas investors may become migrants and actually occupy this housing (along with housing in other countries) since they are affluent. Such individuals, being participants in the global economy, often have economic interests in more than one country. Much of the demand for the high-density component of urban consolidation has, however, been manufactured by developers and by the marketeers and advertisers of such developers. Finally, there is evidence that immigrants in the past have made significant use of dual-occupancy provisions to accommodate close, and often elderly, relatives near to their own family home.

Immigration and social segregation: ghettos and inequality

Critics of an ethnically and culturally diverse immigration flow have argued that social segregation and difference in our cities will (or may) result in social division and the demise of 'one Australia'. This is despite the fact that much recent overseas research has focussed on culture and citizenship and has demonstrated that a well-integrated, cohesive, productive and dynamic nation can arise with cultural, ethnic and linguistic diversity. In fact a productive and dynamic nation is more likely when there is cultural, ethnic and linguistic diversity, as there is in Australia's large cities. Most supporters of cultural and ethnic diversity argue for one law rather than separate legal systems for the different cultures, at least in the Australian situation. While there might be some modification of the law to take account of different religious practices, fundamental rights of individuals, children and adults are recognised. Indeed it is arguable that Australia has not gone far enough, especially at the Local government level in the cities, in the recognition of diversity and difference.

It has commonly been assumed (and taught) that Australian cities contain Little Italies, Little Greeces, Little Macedonias, Little Lebanons and Little Vietnams, following a terminology used early this century in American cities, and enshrined today in tourist brochures and heritage listings. This terminology implied enclaves, and homogeneous ethnic groupings and institutions in particular areas. Even in American cities there was rarely complete ethnic homogeneity at the local level among immigrant-origin populations, although there were (and are) such situations in African-American neighbourhoods in American cities. In Australia, we should not designate as ethno-specific enclaves, Greek, Italian, Lebanese, Chinese or Vietnamese 'ethnic neighbourhoods'.

There are of course quite strong ethnic concentrations or clusters but even in the strongest clusters other immigrant group members and Australian-born persons live. It therefore follows that the word ghetto is entirely misleading and inappropriate for identifying any immigrant-origin community grouping in any Australia city. For a group to be ghettoised the greatest majority of its members

146

must reside in one locality of a city. The majority of the population in that locality must also be comprised of members of that group. Patently this has not taken place with any ethnic group in any Australian city.

It has nevertheless been shown that unemployment levels are higher and incomes lower among ethnic Vietnamese and Chinese from Vietnam, Spanish speakers from Latin America and Moslems from the Middle East, in some areas of residential concentration in Sydney. In part this results from recency of arrival in Australia. In part it is the result of these groups having higher proportions with lesser levels of English proficiency. Many do not have the work skills required for the newer types of jobs being created in Sydney and a great number of manufacturing jobs – which used to provide work for many recent immigrants – have gone with industrial restructuring in inner Sydney and outer western Sydney. There are some parallels in Springvale and other industrial areas of Melbourne. When industrial restructuring takes place, if new jobs *are* created they are likely to require different skills than those possessed by the workers who have been displaced. In western Sydney, many new manufacturing jobs have been created, however their skill base is often different. Particular localities there have experienced persistently higher levels of joblessness, in which 'ethnicity' plays a part, for reasons mentioned. Over 20 years there has been a general increase in the inequality of the overall distribution of income and wealth. It has been suggested that policies of trade liberalisation, deregulation of the economy and labour markets, and privatisation have been accompanied by general increases in inequalities of income and that these distributional inequalities translate into greater spatial inequalities. Research by Hunter and Gregory (1995, 1996) indicates that those suburbs which were originally disadvantaged in socioeconomic terms have become yet more relatively disadvantaged. Many of these suburbs are 'Anglo-Celtic' primarily, but some do have concentrations of more recently arrived migrants from non English-speaking backgrounds. The weight of evidence, however, at least with those from the former Indochina in western Sydney, in areas of strong ethnic concentration, is that despite high unemployment and low incomes, owner occupancy of housing has increased significantly, perhaps through the cooperative benefits that can accrue from ethnic concentration. More research is required, examining change over a long time-frame to study the processes of economic improvements in ethnic concentrations and whether there are specific structural problems resulting from concentration of disadvantage. It is likely, however, that the improvements will outweigh the disadvantages, as the result of the strong motivation for economic betterment that has brought migrants from a great variety of backgrounds to Australia. A considerable potential for entrepreneurship exists within many ethnic communities and within many areas of concentration.

References

Alexander, I. 1981, Post-war metropolitan planning: goals and reality P. Troy (ed.) *Equity in the City*, Allen and Unwin, Sydney

Anderson, K. 1991, *Vancouver's Chinatown, Racial Discourse in Canada, 1875-1980,* McGill-Queens University Press, Montreal.

Anderson, K. 1993, Constructing geographies: race, place and the making of Sydney's Aboriginal Redfern, in P. Jackson and J. Penrose (eds) *Constructions of Race, Place and Nation*, UCL Press, London, pp. 81-99.

Australian Bureau of Statistics (various years: a), *Demography Bulletins*, ABS Canberra.

Australian Bureau of Statistics (various years: b), *Vital Statistics*, ABS Canberra.

Australian Bureau of Statistics (various years: c), *Internal Migration Matrix Tapes*, ABS Canberra.

Australian Bureau of Statistics 1983, *Estimated Resident Population and Components of Change in Population of Local Government Areas (final) NSW 1976-1981*, ABS, NSW Office, Catalogue No. 3208.1.

Australian Bureau of Statistics 1988, *Estimated Resident Population and Components of Change in Population of Statistical Local Areas, NSW 1981 to 1986 (final)*, ABS, NSW Office, Catalogue No. 3208.1.

Australian Bureau of Statistics 1991a, *Community Profile Tables from the 1991 Census of Population and Housing*, AGPS, Canberra.

Australian Bureau of Statistics 1991b, Census of Population and Housing (unpublished labour force data), Canberra.

Australian Bureau of Statistics 1993, *Estimated Resident Population and Components of Change in Population of Statistical Local Areas in New South Wales 1986 to 1991*, ABS, NSW Office, Catalogue No. 3208.1.

Australian Bureau of Statistics 1995, *Australian Demographic Statistics*, AGPS Canberra, Catalogue No. 3101.0.

Australian Bureau of Statistics Census 1991, *Crosstabulation of Birthplace by Language, Religion and Socioeconomic Status, Health Services Language Program* (Consortium), Sydney.

Australian Population and Immigration Council 1973, *A Decade of Migrant Settlement*, AGPS, Canberra.

Australian Urban and Regional Development Review 1995, *Green Cities*, Strategy Paper No. 3, AGPS, Canberra.

Badcock, B. 1995, Towards more equitable cities: a receding prospect? in P. Troy (ed.) *Australian Cities*, Cambridge University Press, Melbourne.

Beer, A. and Cutler, C. 1995, *Atlas of the Australian People – 1991 Census, South Australia*, AGPS, Canberra.

Bell, M. 1995, *Internal Migration in Australia 1986-1991: Overview Report*, AGPS, Canberra.

Bell, M. 1992, *Internal Migration in Australia 1981-86*, AGPS, Canberra.

Bell, M. and Cooper, J. 1995, *Internal Migration in Australia 1986-1991: The Overseas-Born*, AGPS, Canberra.

Birrell, R. 1993, Ethnic concentrations: The Vietnamese experience, *People and Place*, vol. 1, pp. 26-31.

Birrell, R. and Tonkin, S. 1992, Constraints and opportunities for growth: Sydney and Perth compared, ch. 4 in National Population Council, *Population Issues and Australia's Future: Consultants Reports*, AGPS, Canberra.

Blainey, G. 1993, Review and critique of N. Viviani and J. Coughlan, Indochinese in Australia, the issues of unemployment and residential concentration, *BIMPR Bulletin*, no. 10, pp. 25-6.

Burnley, I.H. 1996a, *Atlas of the Australian People – 1991 Census*, AGPS, Canberra.

Burnley, I.H. 1996b, Associations between overseas, intra-urban and internal migration dynamics in Sydney, 1976-91, *Journal of the Australian Population Association*, vol. 13 (in press).

Burnley, I.H. 1994, Immigration, ancestry and residence in Sydney, *Australian Geographical Studies*, vol. 32, pp. 69-89.

Burnley, I. H. 1989, Settlement dimensions of the Vietnam-born population in metropolitan Sydney, *Australian Geographic Studies*, vol. 27, pp. 129-154.

Burnley, I.H. 1985, Acculturation and adjustment of immigrant groups at the neighbourhood level in Sydney, in I.H. Burnley, G. McCall and S. Encel (eds) *Immigration and Ethnicity in the 1980s*, Longman Cheshire, Melbourne.

Burnley, I.H. 1974, The urbanisation of the Australian population, in I.H. Burnley (ed.) *Urbanisation in Australia – The Post-war Experience*, Cambridge University Press, Melbourne.

Burnley, I.H. 1973, Immigrants in Australian cities, *Australian Quarterly*, vol. 44, pp. 15-27.

Burnley, I.H. 1972, European immigration settlement patterns in metropolitan Sydney, 1947-1966, *Australian Geographical Studies*, vol. 10, pp. 61-78.

Burnley, I.H. and Choi, C.Y. 1974, Population components in the growth of cities, in I.H. Burnley (ed.) *Urbanisation in Australia, the Post-war Experience*, Cambridge University Press, Melbourne.

Burnley, I.H. and Forrest, J. 1995, Social impacts of economic restructuring on immigrant groups, *Australian Quarterly*, vol. 67, pp. 69-84.

Burnley, I.H., and Murphy, P.A. 1994, *Immigration, Housing Costs and Population Dynamics in Sydney*, AGPS, Canberra.

Butlin, N.G. 1965, Long run trends in Australian per capita consumption, in K. Hancock (ed.) *The National Income and Social Welfare*, Cheshire, Melbourne.

Campbell, I., Fincher, R. and Webber, M. 1991, Occupational mobility in segmented labour markets: the experience of immigrant workers in Melbourne, *Australian and New Zealand Journal of Social Science*, vol. 27, pp. 172-94.

Castles, S., Collins, J., Gibson, K., Tait, D. and Alcorso, C. 1993, *The Global Milkbar and the Global Sweatshop: Ethnic Small Business and the Economic Restructuring of Sydney*, Centre for Multicultural Studies, University of Wollongong.

Cervero, R. 1995, Changing home-work relationships: implications for metropolitan structure and mobility, in J. Brotchie, M. Batty, E. Blakely, P. Hall and P. Newton (eds) *Cities in Competition*, Longman, Melbourne, ch. 17.

City of Melbourne Strategy Plan 1985, Melbourne City Council, City Strategic Planning Division, Melbourne.

Clarke, H.R., Chisholm, A.H., Edwards, G.W. and Kennedy, J.O.S. 1990, *Immigration, Population and the Environment*, AGPS, Canberra.

Clarke, H.R. and Ng, Y-K, 1993, Immigration, and economic welfare: resource and environmental aspects, *The Economic Record*, vol. 69, pp. 259-73.

Clarke, H.R. and Ng, Y.K. 1991, Are there valid economic grounds for restricting immigration? *Economic Papers*, vol. 10, pp. 71-76.

Collins, J. 1991, Turning off the tap, *Australian Left Review*, No. 134, pp. 34-5

Collins, J., Gibson, K., Alcorso, C., Castles, S. and Tait, D. 1995, *A Shop Full of Dreams: Ethnic Small Business in Australia*, Pluto Press, Sydney.

Collins, J. 1988, *Migrant Hands in Distant Lands: Australia's Post-war Immigration*, Pluto Press, Sydney.

Commonwealth Department of Human Services and Health 1994, *Southern Metropolitan Region* [of Victoria]: *Regional Needs Analysis*, Melbourne.

Commonwealth Grants Commission (CGC) 1995, *Reports on Research in Progress*, 1995, vol. 1, AGPS, Canberra.

Commonwealth Grants Commission (CGC) 1994, *Reports on Research in Progress*, 1994, AGPS, Canberra.

Commonwealth Grants Commission (CGC) 1993, *Report on General Grant Relativities 1993, Volume II – Methods, Assessments and Analysis*, AGPS, Canberra.

Commonwealth Industry Commission 1993, *Taxation and Financial Policy Impacts on Urban Settlement*, Draft Report, vol. 1, AGPS, Canberra.

Commonwealth of Australia (various years), *Censuses of Population and Housing*, ABS, Canberra.

Commonwealth of Australia, Department of Employment, Education and Training 1984-1993, *Small Area Labour Markets Statistics*, AGPS, Canberra.

Croft, A. 1996, Suburbs, women and transport: a case study of Bankstown, unpublished BA (Hons) thesis, Macquarie University.

Cutts, L. 1992, *Immigration and Local Government Budgets*, AGPS, Canberra.

Daly, M.T. 1982, *Sydney Boom, Sydney Bust*, Allen and Unwin, Sydney.

Davison, G. 1993, *The Past and Future of the Australian Suburb, Urban Research Program*, Australian National University, Working Paper No. 33, Canberra.

Davison, G. 1987, The capital cities, in G. Davison and J.W. McCarty (eds) *Australians 1888*, Fairfax, Sime and Weldon, Sydney.

Davidoff, L. and Hall, C. 1987, *Family Fortunes: Men and Women of the English Middle Class, 1750-1850*, Hutchinson, London.

Dawkins, P. 1991, *Flows of Immigrants to South Australia, Tasmania and Western Australia*, AGPS, Canberra.

Day, L.H. 1970, Fertility, in S. Encel and F. Davies (ed.) *Australian Society*, 2nd edn, Cheshire, Melbourne

Dunn, K. 1993, The Vietnamese concentration in Cabramatta, site of avoidance and deprivation or island of adjustment and participation, *Australian Geographical Studies,* vol. 31, pp. 228-45.

Dwyer, L., Burnley, I., Forsyth, P. and Murphy, P. 1993, *Tourism-Immigration Interrelationships*, AGPS, Canberra.

Economic Planning and Advisory Council 1995, *Private Infrastructure Task Force: Interim Report*, AGPS, Canberra.

Economic Planning and Advisory Council 1988, *Economic Infrastructure in Australia*, Council Paper no. 33, AGPS, Canberra.

Fagan, R.H. 1995, Work, settlement and population in Sydney's west, *Geography Bulletin*, vol. 27, pp. 101-11.

Fagan, R. and Webber, M. 1994, *Global Restructuring – The Australian Experience,* Oxford University Press, Melbourne.

Fincher, R. 1991, *Immigration, Urban Infrastructure and the Environment*, AGPS, Canberra.

Fisher, N. 1981, Immigration and the labour market, *Economic Papers*, vol. 674, pp. 1-18.

Forster, C. 1991, *Areas of Multiple Disadvantage in Adelaide,* Planning Review Research Paper No. 15, 2020 Vision, Planning Strategy for Metropolitan Adelaide, State Government of South Australia, Department of Environment and Planning, Adelaide.

Flannery, T 1995, *The Future Eaters*, Reed Books, Melbourne.

Friedmann, J. 1995, The world city hypothesis, in P. Knox and P.J. Taylor (eds) *World Cities in a World System*, Cambridge University Press, Cambridge.

Friedmann, J. 1995, Where we stand: a decade of world city research, in P. Knox and P.J. Taylor (eds) *World Cities in a World System*, Cambridge University Press, Cambridge.

French, J.R.J. 1991, Making the connection, *Search*, vol. 22, pp. 122-3.

Fricker, L. 1978, Some aspects of Melbourne's 19th century urbanisation process, PhD thesis, University of Melbourne.

Frost, L. 1991, *The New Urban Frontier*, UNSW Press, Sydney.

Gosden, R. 1986, Sydney's toxic waste dump – the Pacific, *Chain Reaction*, no. 46, p. 18.

Glynn, S. 1971, *Urbanisation in Australian History*, Nelson, Melbourne.

Greiner, N. 1990, The general economic, budgetary and other effects [of immigration] on New South Wales, Speech by the New South Wales Premier to the National Immigration Outlook Conference, November 16.

Gregory, R. and Hunter, B. 1995, *The Macro Economy and the Growth of Urban Ghettos and Urban Poverty in Australia*, Center for Economic Policy Research, Australian National University, Discussion Paper No. 325, Canberra.

Grimes, S. 1982, Irish friendship networks in metropolitan Sydney, unpublished PhD thesis in Geography, UNSW, Sydney.

Hamnett, S. and Parham, S., 1992, 2020 Vision: a planning strategy for metropolitan Adelaide, *Urban Futures Journal*, vol. 2, pp. 78-85.

Hardin, G. 1968, The tragedy of the commons, *Science*, vol. 162, pp. 1243-48.

Harrison, D. 1984, The impact of immigration on a depressed labour market: the South Australian experience, *Economic Record*, vol. 60, pp. 57-67.

Hollick, M. 1994, Australia's environment, resources and immigration policy in a global context, *Australian Biologist*, vol. 7, pp. 80-90.

House of Representatives Standing Committee on Long Term Strategies 1994, *Australia's Population 'Carrying Capacity'*, AGPS, Canberra.

Hugo, G.J. 1996, *Atlas of the Australian People (1991) Western Australia*, AGPS, Canberra.

Hugo, G. 1995, *Understanding Where Immigrants Live*, AGPS, Canberra.

Hugo, G.J., 1994a, The turnaround in Australia: some first observations from 1991 census, *Australian Geographer*, vol. 25, pp. 1-17.

Hugo, G.J. 1994b, Demographic and spatial aspects of immigration, pp. 30-110 in Wooden, M. et al. (eds) *Australian Immigration, a Survey of the Issues*, 2nd edn, AGPS, Canberra.

Hugo, G.J. 1992, *Atlas of the Australian People (1986) New South Wales*, AGPS, Canberra.

Hugo, G.J. and Maher, C. 1995, *Atlas of the Australian People, 1991, Overview,* AGPS, Canberra.

Hugo, G.J., Rudd, D., and Young, M. 1991, *Future Population Change in Adelaide,* Planning Review Research Paper, State Government of South Australia, Department of Environment and Planning, Adelaide.

Humphries, D. and Sharp, M. 1995, Carr wants migrant intake cut, *Sydney Morning Herald*, 22 May, p. 2.

Hunter, B. and Gregory, R. 1996, An exploration of the relationship between inequality of individual, household and regional inequality in Australian cities, *Urban Policy and Research*, vol. 14, pp. 171-82.

Inglis, P.A. and Stromback, T. 1986, Migrants' unemployment: the determinants of employment success, *Economic Record*, vol. 62, pp. 310-24.

Inglis, C., and Wu, C.T. 1993, The 'new' migration of Asian skills and capital to Australia, in C. Inglis, S. Gunasekaran, G. Sullivan and C.T. Wu (eds) *Asians in Australia: The Dynamics of Migration and Settlement,* Allen and Unwin, Sydney.

Jackson, R. 1996, *Atlas of the Australian People (1991), Queensland* AGPS, Canberra.

Jamrozick, A. 1991, Immigrants and the recession: an expendable labour force? *Migration Action*, vol. 13, pp. 22-8.

Johnston, R.J., Gregory, D. and Smith, D.M. 1994, *The Dictionary of Human Geography*, Blackwell, Oxford.

Junanakar, P.N. and Pope, D. 1993, *Recent Immigrants and Housing*, AGPS, Canberra.

Jupp, J. 1993, Ethnic concentration: a reply to Bob Birrell, *People and Place*, vol. 1, pp. 51-52.

Jupp, J., McRobbie, A. and York, B. 1990, *Metropolitan Ghettoes and Ethnic Concentrations*, The Office of Multicultural Affairs, Canberra, 2 volumes.

Kelly, M. (ed.) 1986, *Sydney: City of Suburbs*, UNSW Press, Sydney.

Kendig, H. 1979, *New Life for Old Suburbs*, Allen and Unwin, Sydney.

Kirwan, R. 1991, *Financing Urban Infrastructure: Equity and Efficiency Considerations*, National Housing Strategy Background Paper No. 4, AGPS, Canberra.

Kirwan, R. 1990, Infrastructure finance: aims, attitudes and approaches, *Urban Policy and Research*, vol. 8, pp. 185-93.

Lack J. and Templeton J. 1995, *Bold Experiment: A Documentary History of Australian Immigration Since 1945*, Oxford University Press, Melbourne.

Lewis, P. 1992, *Immigrants and Interstate Variations in Economic Growth*, AGPS, Canberra.

Lieberson, S. 1963, *Ethnic Patterns in American Cities,* The Free Press of Glencoe, New York.

Logan, J., Taylor-Gooby, P. and Reuter, M. 1992, *Poverty and Inequality*, in S. Fainstein, I. Gordon and M. Harlow (eds) *Divided Cities: New York and London in the Contemporary World*, Blackwell, London.

Loudon, J.C. 1987, *The Suburban Gardener and Villa Companion* (originally Longmans, London, 1938) reprinted Garland Publishing, New York.

Maddock, R. 1993, Economic policy in the 1990s, in A. Hede and S. Prasser (eds) *Policy-Making in Volatile Times*, Hale and Iremonger, Sydney, pp. 98-111.

Maher, C. 1997, *Residential Mobility in Australian Cities*, AGPS, Canberra (in press).

Maher, C. 1994, Housing prices and geographical scale: Australian cities in the 1980s, *Urban Studies*, vol. 31, pp. 5-27.

Maher, C.A. and Stimson, R.J. 1994, *Regional Population Growth in Australia: Nature, Impacts and Implications*, AGPS, Canberra.

Manning, I. (1978), *The Journey to Work*, Allen and Unwin, Sydney.

Marcuse, P. 1996, *Is Australia Different? Globalization and the New Urban Poverty,* Occasional Paper 3, Australian Housing and Urban Research Institute, Melbourne.

Markus, A. 1993, Racism and the recession, *People and Place*, vol. 1, pp. 35-9.

Massey, D. and Denton, N. 1993, *Apartheid American Style*, Harvard UP, Cambridge Mass.

Mathews, R. 1992, *Immigration and State Budgets*, AGPS, Canberra.

McAllister, I. 1991, Migrant unemployment: who suffers? *Migration Action*, vol. 13, pp. 17-21.

Melville, F. 1995, Cambodian migrants in the workforce of western Sydney, unpublished BSc (Hons) thesis in Geography, UNSW, Sydney.

Mercer, D. 1995, Australia's population 'carrying capacity': one nation – two ecologies: a review and assessment, *People and Place*, vol. 3, pp. 23-28.

Mercer, D. 1994, The House of Representatives Inquiry into Australia's Carrying Capacity: a review of submissions, *People and Place*, vol. 2, pp. 14-20.

Metroplan 1990, *Metroplan – A Planning Strategy for the Perth Metropolitan Region*, Western Australian State Government, Department of Planning and Urban Development, Perth.

Metropolitan Adelaide 1992, *2020 Vision Final Report: A Planning System*, Planning Review, June, State Government of South Australia, Department of Environment and Planning, Adelaide.

Metropolitan Adelaide 1991, *2020 Vision, Ideas for Metropolitan Adelaide*, Planning Review, State Government of South Australia, Department of Environment and Planning, Adelaide.

Millett, M. 1996, White Australia alive and kicking, *Sydney Morning Herald*, 19 June, pp. 1, 6.

Millett, M. 1994, Migrant pressure on Sydney will not go away, *Sydney Morning Herald*, July 20, p. 3.

Millett, M. and Armitage, C. 1994, Feds pressed on migrant funds, *Sydney Morning Herald*, 21 July, p. 5.

Ministry for Planning and Environment 1987, *Shaping Melbourne's Future*, Melbourne.

Moore, D. 1993, Australia's carrying capacity: how many people to the acre? Address to the CSIRO Seminar at the National Press Club, Canberra, 7 April 1993, *Significant Speeches*, Winter 1993, pp. 34-39.

Morris, E.E, 1889, *Picturesque Australia*, Cassell, London, 2 vols.

Murphy, P.A. 1995, Immigration and sustainable cities, *Geographical Society of New South Wales, Conference Proceedings*, no. 12, pp. 1-16.

Murphy, P.A. 1993, Immigration and the management of Australian cities, *Urban Studies*, vol. 30, pp. 1501-19.

Murphy, P.A., Burnley, I.H., Harding, H.R., Wiesner, D. and Young, V. 1990, *Impact of Immigration on Urban Infrastructure*, AGPS, Canberra.

Murphy, P. and Watson, S. 1995, Winners, losers and curate's eggs: urban and regional outcomes of Australian economic restructuring, 1971-1991, *Geoforum*, vol. 26, pp. 337-49.

Murphy, P. and Watson, S. 1994, Social polarisation and Australian cities, *International Journal of Urban and Regional Research*, vol. 18, pp. 573-590.

Murphy, P. and Watson, S. 1990, Restructuring of Sydney's central industrial area, *Australian Geographical Studies*, vol. 28, pp. 187-203.

National Housing Strategy 1992, Housing Information Study, AGPS, Canberra.

National Housing Strategy 1991, *The Affordability of Australian Housing*, AGPS, Canberra.

National Population Council 1992, *Population Issues and Australia's Future*, Consultants' Reports, AGPS, Canberra.

National Population Council 1990, *Immigration and Housing in the Major Cities*, AGPS, Canberra.

Neilson Associates 1982, *Study of Immigration and Housing Demand in Sydney*, Australian Population and Immigration Research Program, Canberra.

Neutze, M. 1994, Public and private sector investment, ch. 8 in Australian Urban and Regional Development Review, *Investing in Infrastructure*, Workshop Papers No. 5, AGPS, Canberra.

Newman, P.W.G. and Kenworthy, J. 1989, *Cities and Automobile Dependence: A Sourcebook*, Gower, Aldershot.

Nieuwenhuysen, J. 1990, *New Research on Australian Immigration*, AGPS, Canberra.

NSW Department of Environment and Planning 1985, *Internal Migration: An Exploration of NSW Trends Since 1970*, Sydney.

NSW Department of Planning 1993, *Sydney's Future: A Discussion Paper on Planning the Greater Metropolitan Region*, Sydney.

NSW Environment Protection Authority 1993, *State of the Environment*, Sydney.

NSW Department of Transport 1996, *Trends in Sydney's Travel Patterns*, Issues Paper 96/2, Sydney.

NSW Department of Urban Affairs and Planning 1995, *Journey to Work*, Sydney.

NSW Government 1989 and 1992, *Budget Paper No. 2*, Sydney.

NSW Government 1995, *Cities for the 21st Century: Integrated Urban Management for Sydney, Newcastle, the Central Coast and Wollongong,* Department of Planning, Sydney.

NSW Independent Pricing and Regulatory Tribunal 1996, *Inquiry into the Pricing of Public Passenger Transport Services,* Final Report, Sydney.

NSW Local Government Grants Commission 1995, *Annual Report* 1994/95, Sydney.

NSW State Planning Authority 1968, *Sydney Region Outline Plan,* Sydney.

NSW Valuer General 1976-1991, *House Price Data,* Sydney.

O'Neill, P.M. and Fagan, R.H. 1995, The new regional policy: what chance of success? *Australian Quarterly,* vol. 67, pp. 55-68.

Paris, C. 1993, *Housing Australia,* Macmillan, Melbourne.

Peach, C. 1996, Does Britain have ghettos? *Transactions of the Institute of British Geographers,* New Series, vol. 21, pp. 216-235.

Peck, J. 1996, *Work-Place: The Social Regulation of Labor Markets,* Guildford, New York.

Perron, M. 1993, Australia must develop and populate the north, *BIMPR Bulletin,* no. 10, pp. 5-8.

Price, C.A. 1970, Immigrants, in A.F. Davies and S. Encel (eds) *Australian Society,* 2nd edn, Cheshire, Melbourne.

Queensland Department of Housing, Local Government and Planning 1995, *Recent Population and Housing Trends in Queensland,* Planning Information and Forecasting Unit, Brisbane.

Queensland Department of Housing, Local Government and Planning 1994, *Managing Growth in South East Queensland,* Brisbane.

Quinlan, M. and Lever-Tracy, C. 1990, From labour market exclusion to industrial solidarity: Australian trade union responses to Asian workers, 1830-1988, *Cambridge Journal of Economics,* vol. 14, pp. 159-81.

Rich, D.C., The changing nature and location of work in Australia, *Geography Bulletin,* vol. 27, pp. 59-63.

Richardson, H. 1974, *British Immigration to Australia,* ANU Press, Canberra.

Richardson, H.W. 1973, *Regional Growth Theory,* Macmillan, London.

Roe, J. 1995, Australia, Britain and Migration 1915-1940, *A Study of Desperate Hopes,* Cambridge University Press, Melbourne.

Ruthven, P. 1995, Australia population size and the environment: future options, paper presented at the Third National Immigration and Population Outlook Conference, Adelaide, February 22-24.

Sant, M.E.C., and Simons, P.L.S., 1993, The conceptual basis of counter-urbanisation: critique and development, *Australian Geographical Studies,* vol. 31, pp. 113-125.

Sassen, S. 1991, *The Global City*, Princeton University Press, New Jersey.

Saunders, P. 1994, *Welfare and Inequality*, Cambridge University Press, Melbourne.

Searle, G. 1996, *Sydney as a Global City*, New South Wales Department of Urban Affairs and Planning, Sydney.

Sklair, L. 1995, *Sociology of the Global System*, 2nd edn, Prentice Hall, London.

Sommerlad, J. 1988, *Housing Policy for a Multicultural Australia, Office of Multicultural Affairs*, Canberra.

State Planning Commission of Western Australia 1987, *Planning for the Future of the Perth Metropolitan Region,* Report of the Review Group to the State Planning Commission, State Government of Western Australia, Perth.

Stilwell, F. 1997, *Globalisation and Cities: An Australia Political-Economic Perspective*, Urban Research Program, Working Paper no. 59, Australian National University, Canberra.

Stilwell, F. 1993, *Reshaping Australia: Urban Problems and Policies*, Pluto Press, Sydney.

Stimson, R.J. 1970, European immigration settlement patterns in metropolitan Melbourne, 1947-1961, *Tijdschrift Voor Economische en Social Geografie,* vol. 61, pp. 114-26.

Struik, A. 1994, Housing demand by new immigrants, *BIMPR Bulletin*, no. 12, pp. 72-74.

Tait, D. and Gibson, K. 1987, Economic and ethnic restructuring: an analysis of migrant labour in Sydney', *Journal of Intercultural Studies*, vol. 8, pp. 1-27.

Ten, C.L. 1993, Overpopulation, immigration and the standard of living, *Search*, vol. 22, pp. 126-7.

Tolley, G. and Crihfield, J. 1987, City size and place as policy issues, in E.S. Mills (ed.) *Handbook of Regional and Urban Economics*, vol. II, North Holland, Amsterdam, pp. 1285-1311.

Total Environment Centre 1992, *Newsletter*, vol. 11, pp. 4-5.

Travers Morgan Pty Ltd 1991a, *Determinants of the Prices of Established Housing*, Housing Costs Study No. 3, Australian Building Research Grants Scheme, Canberra.

Travers Morgan Pty Ltd 1991b, *Costs of New Housing Developments*, Housing Costs Study No. 1, Australian Building Research Grants Scheme, Canberra.

Trollope, A., Edward, D.D. and Joyce, B. 1873, *Australia*, UQP, St. Lucia (reprint).

Troy, P. 1995, *The Perils of Urban Consolidation,* Federation Press, Sydney.

Tu, P.N.V. 1991, Are there valid economic grounds for restricting immigration? *Economic Papers*, vol. 10, pp. 91-6.

Viviani, N. 1996, Vietnamese concentrations: a response, *People and Place*, vol. 4, pp. 20-23.

Viviani, N. and Coughlan, J. 1993a, Indochinese in Australia: the issues of unemployment and residential concentration, *BIMPR Bulletin*, no. 8, pp. 21-23.

Viviani, N. and Coughlan, J. 1993b, A response to the critics, *BIMPR Bulletin*, no. 10, p. 46.

Wang, L. 1993, Migration and Settlement of Hong Kong Persons in Metropolitan Sydney, unpublished MA (Hons) thesis in Geography, UNSW, Sydney.

Ward, D. 1982, The ethnic ghetto in the United States: past and present, *Transactions of the Institute of British Geographers*, vol. 7, pp. 257-75.

Whitelaw, J. and Humphries, J.S. 1980, Migrant response to an unfamiliar residential environment, in Burnley, I.H., Pryor, R. and Rowland, D. (eds) *Mobility and Community Change in Australia*, UQP, St. Lucia.

Wilson, W. 1990, Residential relocation and settlement adjustment of Vietnamese refugees in Sydney, *Australian Geographical Studies*, vol. 28, pp. 155-177.

Winship, C. 1977 A re-evaluation of indexes of residential segregation, *Social Forces,* vol. 55, pp. 1058-66.

Withers, G. 1991, *Population Issues and Australia's Future*, Final Report of the Population Issues Committee of the National Population Council, AGPS, Canberra.

Withers, G. and Pope, D. 1985, Immigration and unemployment, *Economic Record*, vol. 61, pp. 554-63.

Wooden, M., Holton, R., Hugo, G. and Sloan, J. (eds) 1994, *Australian Immigration: A Survey of the Issues*, 2nd edn, AGPS, Canberra.

Wooden, M. 1994a, The economic impact of immigration, pp. 111-57 in Wooden, M. et al. *Australian Immigration: A Survey of the Issues*, 2nd edn, AGPS, Canberra.

Wooden, M. 1994b, The labour market experience of immigrants, pp. 218-79 in M. Wooden et al. *Australian Immigration: A Survey of the Issues*, 2nd edn, AGPS, Canberra.

Wooden, M. et al. 1994c *Australian Immigration: A Survey of the Issues*, 2nd edn, AGPS, Canberra.

Woods, R.I. 1976, Aspects of the scale problem in the calculation of segregation indices: London and Birmingham, 1961 and 1971, *Tijdschrift Voor Economische en Social Geografie,* vol. 67, pp. 169-74.

Young, C. 1988, Towards a population policy: myths and misconceptions concerning the demographic effects of immigration, *Australian Quarterly*, vol. 60, pp. 220-30.

Zarsky, L. 1991, Ecology, ethics and immigration – a global view, *Search*, vol. 22, pp. 124-5.

Zubrzycki, J.,1964, *Settlers of the Latrobe Valley,* ANU Press, Canberra.

Zunz, O. 1982, *The Changing Face of Inequality: Urbanization, Industrial Development and Immigrants in Detroit, 1880-1920*, University of Chicago Press, Chicago.

Index

Affordable housing, *see* Housing prices

Air pollution levels and trends in Sydney, 103-104

Asia-Australia connections, 5-7
shares of Asian immigrants attracted to Sydney and Melbourne, 7
see also Education exports

Australian Urban and Regional Development Review, 98

Beach pollution in Sydney, 100-101

Bond Scheme to influence the location choices of immigrants, 137-139
see also Regional development

Bureau of Immigration, Multicultural and Population Research, 7

Cabramatta, 36
see also Ethnic concentrations

Canada immigration rate, 2

Chinatowns, 50
social 'construction' of, 50-52
see also Ethnic concentrations

City size, 108-109
see also Regional development

Commonwealth government, *see* Government

Commonwealth Grants Commission, 62, 64
see also Infrastructure

Cultural effects of immigration, 5
implications for trade, 6
pace of change, 5, 9

Cultural significance of immigrant places, 54

Decentralisation, *see* Regional development

De-industrialisation, *see* Economic restructuring

Economic effects at the national level, 2-4, 117-118
ageing of population, 118
demand stimulation for housing, cars and consumer durables, 2-3, 117
expansion of domestic market for goods and services, 3
inflation, 4
labour force expansion, 2, 117
manufacturing labour force, 2, 117
see also Labour markets

Economic restructuring, 8, 117, 122

Education exports, 6-7

Emigration from Australia, 2

Employment issues, *see* Labour markets

Environmental management, 10, 96-112
compensating for negative equity effects of externality pricing, 111
conflicting interests complicate environmental management, 111, *see also* Interest groups
controlling human behaviour to improve urban environmental quality, 107
controlling urban form to improve environmental quality, 104-107
controlling population growth to improve urban environmental quality, 108-109